Ben Affleck

Ben Affleck

Titles in the People in the News series include:

Tim Allen	Madonna
Drew Barrymore	Dominique Moceanu
Tony Blair	Rosie O'Donnell
Bono	The Osbournes
Garth Brooks	Brad Pitt
Sandra Bullock	Colin Powell
George W. Bush	Princess Diana
Nicolas Cage	Prince William
Jim Carrey	Christopher Reeve
Michael Crichton	Julia Roberts
Tom Cruise	The Rolling Stones
Matt Damon	J.K. Rowling
Johnny Depp	Adam Sandler
Celine Dion	Arnold Schwarzenegger
Eminem	Will Smith
Michael J. Fox	Britney Spears
Bill Gates	Steven Spielberg
Mel Gibson	R.L. Stine
John Grisham	Sting
Tom Hanks	John Travolta
Jesse Jackson	Jesse Ventura
Michael Jackson	Robin Williams
Michael Jordan	Oprah Winfrey
Stephen King	Reese Witherspoon
Jennifer Lopez	Elijah Wood
George Lucas	Tiger Woods

PEOPLE
IN THE NEWS

Ben Affleck

by John F. Wukovits

**LUCENT
BOOKS** ®

THOMSON

✦

GALE ™

San Diego • Detroit • New York • San Francisco • Cleveland
New Haven, Conn. • Waterville, Maine • London • Munich

© 2004 by Lucent Books. Lucent Books is an imprint of The Gale Group, Inc.,
a division of Thomson Learning, Inc.

Lucent Books® and Thomson Learning™ are trademarks used herein under license.

For more information, contact
Lucent Books
27500 Drake Rd.
Farmington Hills, MI 48331-3535
Or you can visit our Internet site at http://www.gale.com

LIBRARY OF CONGRESS CATALOGING-IN-PUBLICATION DATA

Wukovits, John F., 1944–
    Ben Affleck / by John F. Wukovits.
        p. cm. — (People in the news)
    ISBN 1-59018-323-1 (lib. bdg. : alk. paper)
    1. Affleck, Ben, 1972– —Juvenile literature. 2. Motion picture actors and actresses—
United States—Biography—Juvenile literature. I. Title. II. Series: People in the news (San
Diego, Calif.)
    PN2287.A435W85 2004
    791.4302'8'092—dc22
                                                    2004000380

Printed in the United States of America

Table of Contents

Foreword

FAME AND CELEBRITY are alluring. People are drawn to those who walk in fame's spotlight, whether they are known for great accomplishments or for notorious deeds. The lives of the famous pique public interest and attract attention, perhaps because their experiences seem in some ways so different from, yet in other ways so similar to, our own.

Newspapers, magazines, and television regularly capitalize on this fascination with celebrity by running profiles of famous people. For example, television programs such as *Entertainment Tonight* devote all of their programming to stories about entertainment and entertainers. Magazines such as *People* fill their pages with stories of the private lives of famous people. Even newspapers, newsmagazines, and television news frequently delve into the lives of well-known personalities. Despite the number of articles and programs, few provide more than a superficial glimpse at their subjects.

Lucent's People in the News series offers young readers a deeper look into the lives of today's newsmakers, the influences that have shaped them, and the impact they have had in their fields of endeavor and on other people's lives. The subjects of the series hail from many disciplines and walks of life. They include authors, musicians, athletes, political leaders, entertainers, entrepreneurs, and others who have made a mark on modern life and who, in many cases, will continue to do so for years to come.

These biographies are more than factual chronicles. Each book emphasizes the contributions, accomplishments, or deeds that have brought fame or notoriety to the individual and shows how that person has influenced modern life. Authors portray their subjects in a realistic, unsentimental light. For example, Bill Gates—the cofounder and chief executive officer of the software giant Microsoft—has been instrumental in making personal computers the most vital tool of the modern age. Few dispute his business savvy, his perseverance, or his technical expertise, yet critics say he is ruthless in his dealings with competitors and driven more by his desire to maintain Microsoft's dominance in the computer industry than by an interest in furthering technology.

In these books, young readers will encounter inspiring stories about real people who achieved success despite enormous obstacles. Oprah Winfrey—the most powerful, most watched, and wealthiest woman on television today—spent the first six years of her life in the care of her grandparents while her unwed mother sought work and a better life elsewhere. Her adolescence was colored by promiscuity, pregnancy at age fourteen, rape, and sexual abuse.

Each author documents and supports his or her work with an array of primary and secondary source quotations taken from diaries, letters, speeches, and interviews. All quotes are footnoted to show readers exactly how and where biographers derive their information and provide guidance for further research. The quotations enliven the text by giving readers eyewitness views of the life and accomplishments of each person covered in the People in the News series.

In addition, each book in the series includes photographs, annotated bibliographies, timelines, and comprehensive indexes. For both the casual reader and the student researcher, the People in the News series offers insight into the lives of today's newsmakers—people who shape the way we live, work, and play in the modern age.

Introduction

"I Value All Those Guys More"

FAME HAS BEEN a two-edged sword for actor Ben Affleck. On the one hand, his starring roles in such hit movies as *Good Will Hunting, Armageddon,* and *The Sum of All Fears* have brought him wealth, public adulation, a high profile in entertainment media, and respect within the industry. On the other hand, this intelligent man, whose voracious reading tastes include classic literature as well as best sellers, struggles with the lack of privacy that accompanies Hollywood notoriety. He is an example of an individual who rose to stardom from humble beginnings and who pays a heavy price in relinquishing what most people take for granted.

His life also shows that family and friends, not big-budget films and national adulation, bring stability and happiness. From his earliest moments in Cambridge, Massachusetts, Affleck shared a warm family life with his mother and younger brother. Though raised in adolescence by his mother—his parents divorced when Affleck was twelve—the future actor eventually developed a close bond with his father. When Affleck first appeared in television commercials and children's shows, his mother stood at his side, figuratively and literally, to make sure that he did not grow into a "difficult" child actor who demands preferential treatment and is vulnerable to diverse problems in the rough adjustment from childhood to adulthood.

In addition to his nurturing family environment, Affleck also benefited from a corps of closely knit friends. He first met most of these buddies in elementary school, and even today, more than twenty years later, many photographs of Affleck appearing in the nation's newspapers and magazines include one or more of his childhood friends. Though he is certainly in the celebrity spotlight, Affleck is basically an average guy who enjoys hanging out

Ben Affleck has achieved fame beyond his wildest dreams. Despite his celebrity status, Affleck claims to find happiness in his relationships with family and friends.

with friends at a local bar or attending a Boston Red Sox baseball game.

Ben Affleck reserves his trust for his family and longtime pals, whom he counts on for stability and security when the stress of publicity peaks. The most recent evidence of this came in connection with his rocky relationship with actress Jennifer Lopez,

Affleck, the Fortune-Teller?

Did Ben Affleck unwittingly predict the difficulties he would experience with Jennifer Lopez? In 1998, long before Affleck and Lopez's romance dominated the headlines, interviewer Luaine Lee of E! Online asked Affleck if he would ever star in a romantic film involving a woman with whom he had a serious relationship. Affleck declared the probability was low, as he believed it would be too difficult. He said he would "hate to do a straight-up romantic movie with somebody with whom I was involved. I just think that would be whoring your personal romantic life for the sake of your professional life."

Five years later, the media had a field day reporting the on-again, off-again romance and wedding of Affleck and Lopez, who had just seen their 2003 romantic film, *Gigli*, sink under a wave of negative reviews.

Affleck and Jennifer Lopez pose at the premiere of their 2003 film Gigli, *a box-office disaster.*

an episode that dominated headlines for months and threatened to smother his individuality.

Bennifer, Not Ben Affleck

The media frenzy surrounding Affleck's relationship with Jennifer Lopez matched or surpassed anything the young actor had ever experienced. Reporters and photographers staked out popular Los Angeles restaurants and nightclubs in hopes of catching glimpses of the young, good-looking couple. Every move the pair made seemed to eventually make its way into the pages of one entertainment publication or another or garner top headlines in a nightly Hollywood news television show.

As if to show that the couple had even lost control over their own names, the press had created nicknames for the duo. They were not Ben and Jennifer; they were, instead, Bennifer, Ben-Lo, or Jennufleck. Their individual identities were blended until they seemed to exist only in terms of each other.

The pair met in December 2001 while filming the movie *Gigli*, and fast became a couple, openly patronizing restaurants and parties together. Speculation heated the following July when Lopez filed for divorce from husband Chris Judd, only two months before Affleck took her to his childhood home in Boston to meet his mother. A $3.5 million pink diamond adorning her left hand confirmed that the couple had become officially engaged. The romance continued to unfold in public into 2003, when the couple purchased a $7 million Georgia mansion and presented Oscars at the annual Academy Awards show.

Every move the couple made, together or apart, was presented as evidence that they were about to marry or about to break up. If Lopez flew alone to visit family or friends, reporters wondered if the relationship had ended. If Affleck joined his buddies for a night on the town, headlines predicted dire times for the couple.

A Blip on the Radar?

A media backlash against the couple exploded with the 2003 release of *Gigli*, a romantic comedy pairing the couple on-screen for the first time. Critics savaged the film. A reviewer in the *Los Angeles Times* claimed *Gigli* was "nearly as unwatchable as it is unpronounceable,"[1] and Richard Roeper of the *Washington Post* labeled it one of the worst movies he had ever seen. One movie patron emerging from a screening of the film told *USA Today* that despite being a couple offscreen, Affleck and Lopez so miserably failed to create any chemistry on-screen that he started to nod off in the middle of the movie.

Affleck admitted that he had doubts about the movie before it reached theaters. He and other key participants, such as the writers, attempted to fashion a better film, but as he told *Variety* magazine, "it was like putting a fish's tail on a donkey's head."[2]

First-week results confirmed the movie's plight. Industry analysts expected that the opening weekend gross receipts for a film with two major stars such as Affleck and Lopez would total $11 million, but *Gigli* barely pulled in $4 million. The film, which cost $54 million to make, quickly sank into oblivion.

Predictions from film critics filled newspapers, television shows, and magazines. Some declared that Ben Affleck and Jennifer Lopez would fade as quickly as their movie. Others stated that *Gigli* represented yet another in a string of Affleck film failures, and that the only way he could remain in the business was to star in a hit film.

Affleck's spokesman, Ken Sunshine, defended Affleck and brushed aside talk of his demise as grossly premature. "This is a blip on the radar," stated Sunshine. "One movie that tanked and some insanity in the tabloids. Everyone in the real world knows that it's nonsense."[3] Sunshine added that Affleck had already finished three forthcoming films that would propel him back to the top.

"A Celebrity of a Completely Different Magnitude"

Meanwhile, Affleck had to weather the constant media attention focused on his personal relationship with Lopez, one of the most photographed women in the industry. Headlines blared news of their upcoming nuptials, columnists described the gown selected by the bride and the engagement ring bestowed by the groom, and fans collected in throngs wherever the pair appeared. His celebrity was a stark contrast to his working-class roots, but he ap-

Don't Believe Everything You Read, Mom

Media coverage sensationalizes celebrities' lives, often spreading gossip without verifying the story. Ben Affleck understands that this publicity is a part of his life as a movie star, but sometimes the people close to him have a more difficult time.

During the late 1990s, when Affleck was dating Gwyneth Paltrow, columnists and industry observers wondered when the couple would marry. Periodically, reports floated that the two had quietly tied the knot. Affleck's mother read such a report and telephoned her son to ask if indeed he had married without telling her. In a 1999 interview, Affleck told *Playboy* magazine he could barely believe his mother had fallen for the tale. "Mom," an incredulous Affleck said, "if I were married, don't you think I would have called you? Are we on the outs? I mean, don't you think you might have been there?"

Affleck's words eased his mother's mind, but the incident shows what some movie stars must accept if they intend to be major players in Hollywood.

peared to take it in stride. If he felt like a piece of paper in the midst of a hurricane, he never showed it in public.

The wedding hype ended at the same time as *Gigli*'s debut. Rumors that the pair had broken up presaged the actual event. A few rumbles of discontent reached the news, then more as the days passed. Affleck, the rumors stated, sought more privacy than his world with Lopez permitted. He wanted a return to his bachelor days, when he and his school buddies from Boston, including fellow actor Matt Damon, drank and caroused together with little more on their minds but what bar would be their next destination.

"He's a big star, but she's a celebrity of a completely different magnitude," a source close to Affleck told *Us* magazine. "[This whole incident] didn't surprise anyone who knows them. Ben should have known what he was getting into. When you enter the world of Jennifer Lopez, your life becomes very public."[4]

The circus reached new heights on September 9, 2003, when the couple announced the postponement of their wedding, claiming the media frenzy had tossed all plans into disarray. Rumors and speculation about the cause of the relationship's apparent end spread rapidly.

Fellow actor Matt Damon has been Affleck's closest friend since childhood. The pair rose together from obscurity to become two of Hollywood's biggest names.

"I Value All Those Guys More"

As he always has, whether in moments of triumph or in moments of distress, Ben Affleck again turned to what serves as the anchor in his life, the factor that lends stability in the midst of so much chaos—Boston and his friends. During these hectic times he flew home to be with family and a group of pals he has known since childhood, people who knew the emerging Ben Affleck and understand that what he needs most is loyalty, companionship, and honesty, not fame and adulation.

"He would roll his eyes anytime his friends brought up the wedding," said a close friend to *Us* magazine. "He wasn't acting like a guy in love."[5] Back home, in comfortable surroundings, Affleck could relax, secure that what he said or did remained hidden from prying public eyes. While the vast majority of people leave childhood friends behind and move on to new associates and new experiences, Affleck does the reverse. The more fame he earns, the more tightly he appears to hold on to his roots.

Most of all, he benefited from the company of his closest friend, Matt Damon, a buddy with whom he shared his dreams of the future during high school cafeteria talks and whose successful acting and writing career has been so closely linked to Affleck's. The pair share experiences that neither Affleck's parents nor his other friends understand, for both entered the crucible of Hollywood fame together.

"We're probably better friends now," Affleck told a magazine reporter in an extensive interview. "We're able to bounce stuff off each other. I think we value our friendship more and understand how rare it is to have a good friend. There's a small group of guys I've known since I was a kid. I value all those guys more. Obviously Matt in particular, because we have a common experience."[6]

That common experience started in a working-class neighborhood in the midst of one of the nation's most revered educational climates. Harvard University and the Massachusetts Institute of Technology vied for space with local taverns and bars, middle-class houses, and public schools. All of it influenced the young Ben Affleck.

Chapter 1

"The Coolest Thing I've Ever Seen"

T HE YOUTHFUL BEN AFFLECK exhibited few of the traits that would one day propel him to Hollywood fame. His childhood was much like that of most youngsters in a middle-class, suburban neighborhood populated mainly by factory workers and people accustomed to laboring with their hands. He played baseball with buddies, performed without distinction in elementary school, and faced moments of sadness amid happiness.

Fortunately his parents were strong positive influences. He gained strength of character and a sense of responsibility from his mother, while his father showed Ben that life offers much joy despite pain. From them, Ben developed both a childlike enthusiasm for the theater and a serious, adultlike attitude. Both traits played a role in fashioning the Ben Affleck who later occupied so prominent a position in American film.

A Love for Cambridge

Benjamin Geza Affleck was born on August 15, 1972, in Oakland, California, to parents of Scotch-Irish ancestry. His mother, Chris, was an elementary school teacher; his father, Timothy, drifted in and out of a variety of jobs.

The family briefly lived in Berkeley, California, before moving to Massachusetts when Affleck was two years old. A year later, Ben's brother, Casey, was born. In 1977 the clan once again packed its belongings and headed to a working-class neighborhood in Cambridge, home to world-renowned Harvard University and the Massachusetts Institute of Technology (MIT), both top-ranked academic institutions.

Cambridge instantly captivated Ben Affleck. He and his pals from the local public school followed all the local professional sports teams, and especially marveled at the feats of Carl Yastrzemski of the Boston Red Sox and Larry Bird of the Boston Celtics. When not intent on a pickup game of baseball or basketball, Affleck rushed to theaters to see the latest fare. He absorbed the summer blockbusters like *Star Wars*, *Jaws*, and *Back to the Future*, often waiting impatiently in line to slip into the theater, and soon possessed an impressive array of action figures based on the films. Darth Vader, the imposing villain from the *Star Wars* films, both frightened and fascinated him.

As soon as he was old enough to appreciate it, he reveled in the town's culture. Bookstores, college campuses, and intellectual pursuits occupied center stage, stimulating his lifelong passion for books. He read voraciously, a habit he continues to this day.

Affleck grew up in a working-class neighborhood in Cambridge, Massachusetts, where he enjoyed playing baseball and catching the latest movies.

A Bumpy Childhood

At the same time he felt a gap between the students who attended Harvard and MIT and himself. The students, many of whom came from wealthy families, were getting what many considered the best education in the country while he lived in a modest neighborhood of a working-class section standing in the shadows of Harvard. It was almost as if an invisible, but palpable, line sepa-

Harvard University

Harvard University, which plays such an important part in both Ben Affleck's and Matt Damon's lives, is the oldest institution of higher learning in the United States. Founded in 1636, only sixteen years after the arrival of the Pilgrims at Plymouth, the university has expanded from nine students to the current enrollment of more than eighteen thousand degree candidates.

Many distinguished individuals have attended Harvard. Bill Gates started his college career in the Cambridge institution, and seven presidents of the United States—John Adams, John Quincy Adams, Rutherford B. Hayes, Theodore and Franklin D. Roosevelt, John F. Kennedy, and George W. Bush—received degrees from Harvard.

The school played a key role in *Good Will Hunting*. Damon wrote the script for one of his professors, he and Affleck acted out an early scene at Harvard, and university life forms a central portion of the film.

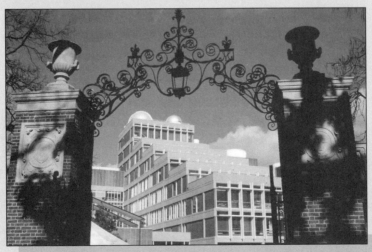

Affleck and Damon chose Harvard University as the setting for their successful film Good Will Hunting.

rated the youth of Cambridge from the students who annually flooded into the town each fall to attend the elite academic institutions, then departed each spring. At times, he wished he were one of those fortunate students, but mostly he, like most of his childhood friends, felt that the collegians were arrogant invaders intent on asserting their superiority over the local inhabitants.

Ben noticed the chasm dividing the diverse worlds. After all, his father struggled at a number of jobs some people considered menial. Timothy Affleck, an educated man with a love for the theater, never seemed to settle into an occupation to which he was well suited. At various times he held a string of short-lived jobs as a janitor at Harvard University, an auto mechanic, and a bartender.

Affleck's father unsuccessfully tried to balance the strain of earning enough money to provide for his family with his desire to perform in local theater. He loved the acting profession, but at the same time he had the responsibility to put food on the table for his growing family. These diverse interests pulled him in opposite directions, resulting in arguments with his wife, Chris, tension at home, and a general feeling of unhappiness.

Working as a bartender proved to be a bad fit for Timothy. Already facing the usual burdens of raising a family as well as struggling to make a mark in the theater, he more frequently turned to alcohol to relieve stress. Arguments with his wife while drunk affected their older son, who yearned for tranquility instead of the harsh words he heard at home. Ben Affleck coped with the situation by associating with a large group of school friends and by escaping into books.

He also took note of his father's passion for acting. Instead of watching a weary man returning from the rigors of work, whenever his father headed off to the theater Ben saw an invigorated adult ready to take on new challenges. What was more, his father must have been good at what he did, for he landed roles with the prestigious Theater Company of Boston, where he worked with such noted actors as Oscar winners Dustin Hoffman, Robert Duvall, and Jon Voight.

More and more, Ben Affleck carefully observed that world, and before long he, too, had become hooked on the acting profession. He explained to *Biography* magazine, "My father had a theater background—he worked with a theater company in Boston before I was born. He and my mom had a lot of friends who were actors, and I was around them all the time and it rubbed off."[7]

"Absolutely What I Wanted to Do"

It did not take long for Affleck to make his initial mark in acting, albeit on a small scale. In 1978 the six-year-old appeared in a television commercial promoting Burger King products.

This job, and the connections made by his parents, led to additional work. The next year one of his mother's friends, independent filmmaker Jan Egleson, needed a young boy for a part in a movie. Titled *The Dark End of the Street*, the movie depicted life in South Boston and was to be filmed in the city. Affleck's mother offered Ben's services, and as quickly as that, the youth headed to his first audition.

The audition was hardly an arduous process, in which actors and actresses typically vie for limited roles against hundreds of competitors by acting out a part selected by a producer. Ben, ignorant of the long odds against him, walked in, performed the audition, and got the part.

"It sounded like fun to me," he explained of his initial test. "I remember going on an audition and thinking I had a pretty good chance to get the role, having no conception of how it works. I was like, 'Oh you audition and then you do it,' never understanding there might be 500 other kids. So I got the part. Later on I learned that you don't always get what you read for."[8]

Ben benefited from his ignorance of the selection process. Because he did not realize the odds against him, he walked in with confidence, read his scene, and landed the part. Had he grasped ahead of time the importance of his audition, who knows what might have happened.

Typically for a youngster, a star-struck Ben fell in love with what he saw. Actors, actresses, director, and locations fascinated him. "I thought, 'This is the coolest thing I've ever seen,'" he said in a 2002 interview. "It was so much fun. Ever since then, it's absolutely what I wanted to do."[9]

His parents, better understanding the risks and hard work involved, discouraged Ben's interest in a film career. They did not

The 1979 film The Dark End of the Street *depicted the harsh realities of life in South Boston. At the age of seven, Ben won a small part in the movie.*

forbid him to take a more active role, but they pointed out that hundreds of hopefuls enter the business intent on gaining stardom, only to face years of rejection and subsistence wages.

They agreed to let him pursue professional acting, but only during summer months when it would not interfere with school. His mother insisted that he experience as normal a life as possible and was determined that he not turn into a spoiled brat. They started slowly, allowing him to do a few commercials in the Boston area, then let him head to New York for films.

The Voyage of the Mimi

His first big break occurred in 1980, when he landed the role of C.T. Granville, the host of a PBS schoolchildren's series called *The Voyage of the Mimi*. The series, set on a boat called *Mimi*, presented educational episodes about science and the men and women who work in the field. The ten dollars a day allotted out of his pay by his mother seemed like a fortune to eight-year-old Ben, who quickly "invested" the fortune in comic books.

The show filmed segments on location, requiring Ben to travel. His mother always accompanied him, intent on both ensuring that he enjoy as normal a childhood as possible and that he not think he was better than anyone else. "My mom was very concerned that I have a normal childhood," Affleck recalls: "I went to school and only worked sporadically. We were never the family that moved to L.A. because the kid was supporting them."[10]

In many ways, Ben enjoyed a stable home life. Though his father's excessive drinking sometimes caused problems, Ben's mother provided the necessary anchor in his life. Combined with the security of a large group of neighborhood chums, Ben had a solid foundation. In times of stress later in his life, he would often return to these roots as a means of restoring sanity.

The only time Affleck's mother allowed him to work on the set alone was during *The Voyage of the Mimi*'s second season (filmed a few years after the first), when the entire cast and crew traveled to Mexico to film the full season of episodes. She accompanied him south of the border, but in the middle of taping she had to return to Massachusetts because of a serious case of pneu-

Affleck's mother Chris introduced her son to acting, and she has been supportive throughout his career.

monia. The producers promised to look after the eighth grader, so a bit uneasy over the situation but believing she had no alternative, Chris Affleck boarded an airplane bound for the United States.

Chris Affleck did not learn until much later that the producers reneged on their pledge. Occupied with the task of making the show, they barely checked on the youthful actor. As long as he appeared each day and knew his lines, they were satisfied. Ben could not have been happier. He faced a predicament that most teenagers could only dream about—he was free from parental control, living in an exotic foreign nation, with spending money in hand. Ben took complete advantage.

"I was pretty much on my own down there, getting into trouble," he told *Biography* magazine. "I was earning money and I had my own hotel room; I thought I was all grown-up and had all the answers."[11]

By the time he entered high school, Affleck had worked in enough commercials and television productions to gain an insider's view of the business. He enjoyed every minute—mingling with other actors, working with directors, traveling to distant locations. He was also mature enough to realize that he should not let a unique opportunity slip by, and set out to study every facet of the industry. He peppered directors, scriptwriters, and anyone else with questions about what they did and how they did it. He was determined to learn as much as he could so that he could benefit from it later.

To High School

In 1986 the high school freshman won his biggest role to date when the American Broadcasting Company (ABC) signed him to play the key role of Danny in the after-school television special *Wanted: The Perfect Guy.* The story centered around a boy—played by Ben Affleck—trying to find a husband for his mother, played by Madeline Kahn. This movie gave Ben his first opportunity to perform in a key role, as well as learn from an established film star. Kahn had gained acclaim for her work in major Hollywood projects, especially two comedies produced by Mel Brooks, *Young Frankenstein* and *Blazing Saddles.* Ben had made a major leap from

Acquiring an Agent

Ben Affleck helped his good friend Matt Damon sign with the same agency that represented him. Although he had not personally met an agent from the firm—all the work had been done over the telephone and through the mail—Affleck felt confident that he could assist his friend. The process, though, did not go as he expected.

When Affleck and Damon boarded the train for New York City, they imagined the agency would reflect the splendor and drama of the industry. They quickly received an indication that all was not as they thought it would be. Instead of a majestic-looking office building in an exclusive area, they walked into a tiny room housing an elderly man and woman. When they asked to see the agent, instead of a man or woman in an impeccable business suit, the graying couple explained they represented Affleck. What was more, they did not recognize his name since Affleck had been hired for earlier jobs through his auditions, not from any referrals the couple made.

The final letdown came when Affleck wondered if the pair would also represent Damon. No great flurry of promises or grand schemes of success came. According to Matt Damon, as recorded in Chris Nickson's 1999 biography, *Matt Damon: An Unauthorized Biography*, the couple simply replied, with an eye-opening lack of emotion, "Oh yeah, we'll represent Matt too."

With that less than inspiring start, Affleck and Damon began their combined journey to Hollywood.

the PBS series into the larger arena of film productions. He now stood in a new world from which he could learn the acting craft.

Joining Ben in his journey was a close friend who lived only two blocks away. Although Ben enjoyed an earlier start in movies than his cohort Matt Damon, the pair quickly became an inseparable team.

Chapter 2

"Matt and I Had Identical Interests"

As BEN PASSED through high school, more hurdles threatened to deter the young man from what eventually became an acclaimed acting career. The taunts of fellow students, the worries of family, and the hardships of establishing himself in an industry that offered little sympathy to those who could not immediately prove their worth would be daunting to anyone. But in one of Ben's closest childhood friends, he had an ally. The two blended so well that they shared their dreams for the future, plotted courses by which they might attain their dreams, supported one another in their endeavors, and lent comfort when conditions soured. Without Matt Damon's friendship, Ben Affleck's path to Hollywood would have been far more arduous.

Joined at the Hip

Ben Affleck first met Matt Damon when Ben was eight years old. Damon, two years older than Affleck, lived two blocks away in the same Cambridge neighborhood and attended the same elementary school. Their mothers knew each other from their work in education, and Ben recalls first hearing of Matt through his mother. He did not at first receive a good impression, as Chris used to toss Matt in his face as an example of how he should behave.

"My mom was trying to get me to do more work around the house and would say, 'Well, Matt's mom makes *him* cook once a week,'" explained Affleck to *Biography Today*. "So I first knew him as a guy who was really setting a bad precedent in the neighborhood."[12]

Once Ben met Matt, he quickly abandoned his negative opinions. The two hit it off instantly, both in and out of school. Together

Matt Damon

Ben Affleck's best friend was born October 8, 1970, in Cambridge, Massachusetts. His father, Kent, worked in the banking profession, while his mother, Nancy, was a college professor.

Like Affleck, Damon always intended to be an actor. After signing with Affleck's agent, he slowly started landing roles. He made his first major film appearance in 1988's *Mystic Pizza*, which also featured a young Julia Roberts.

Four years later, Damon costarred in *School Ties*, along with Ben Affleck and Brendan Fraser. This led to the film *Geronimo: An American Legend*, which gave him the chance to act with a man he considered one of Hollywood's greatest—Robert Duvall. In 1996's *Courage Under Fire*, Damon lost forty pounds so that he looked more like the heroin addict he portrayed.

Following the success of *Good Will Hunting*, Damon's profile in high-budget films soared. His appearance as Private Ryan in Steven Spielberg's powerful WWII movie *Saving Private Ryan* cemented Damon's grip on stardom, a hold he strengthened with *The Talented Mr. Ripley*, *Ocean's Eleven*, and *The Bourne Identity*.

Like Affleck, Matt Damon dreamed of becoming an actor early in life.

they played games such as Dungeons and Dragons, read every comic book in sight, hurried to nearby theaters to catch the latest Hollywood offerings, and joined the local Little League baseball team. "If one kid had enough for a candy bar," Affleck recalls, "then the candy bar was bought and split in half—that's just the way it's been."[13]

Ben forged such a close bond with Matt in part because Matt became the older brother Ben never had. Matt was his protector, the one the shy Ben could look up to. Damon remembers instances where Affleck would sheepishly walk up to his house, quickly ring the doorbell, then huddle across the street and wait for Damon to appear because he was frightened of a group of kids at the school next door to Damon's home.

The two were constantly together. If a friend spotted one, he was likely to see the other close by. Matt even accompanied Ben on a few auditions for acting, loved what he witnessed, and with the help of Ben's agent, landed a few parts of his own. From then on, their names would be linked both personally and professionally.

"Matt and I had identical interests, so whether we ended up successful or making hot dogs at Dodgers games, we knew we'd end up doing the same sort of things. The remaining friends part was pretty consistent. We saw each other all the time, we talked on the phone all the time."[14]

"I Was Way Too Sensitive"

Ben followed Matt into Cambridge Rindge and Latin School, a prestigious public school adjoining Harvard Square. Immediately, Ben experienced more difficulties than his friend, who seemed to achieve high marks with ease and gain the attention of a bevy of girls. He performed acceptably in the classroom, but never earned the high grades Matt earned. Among their fellow students, Matt was known as the warrior for his tendency to charge toward what he wanted, in and out of the classroom, while Ben was the clown, the one with a less serious nature who rarely put full effort into his school assignments.

There was a simple explanation—Ben did not study as hard as he should have because he hated nuts-and-bolts classwork. He loved reading on his own; then he could determine the interests

Yearbook photos show Affleck and Damon as high school seniors at Cambridge Rindge and Latin School, where the two were self-described "theater nerds."

and ideas he could pursue. In a classroom, however, he lost that control. The teacher determined what was important for Ben. He often wondered why he had to sit through so many classes he considered useless and what value they might have for his future. He usually found no satisfactory answer.

Meeting girls was a similar matter: The more sociable Damon often carried conversations while the timid Affleck remained in the background. He felt he was not as good-looking as Damon nor as confident in dealing with matters of the heart. This did not improve in his freshman year when the first girl for whom he developed a crush dumped him after a brief relationship.

Affleck's shyness intensified in his junior year when he suddenly grew an entire foot in height. Since the rest of his body could not keep up with the rapid growth—his shins, elbows, and knees constantly ached—Affleck walked awkwardly through the school's halls, a fact that did not escape the notice of male and female students alike.

"I don't think the ladies were saying, 'I'm looking for somebody awkward and beanpole-like, who doesn't have control of his own limbs,'" stated Affleck. "My head was misshapen and lumpy, and I was way too sensitive."[15]

Like students in high schools throughout the country, Affleck faced the same obstacles all young adults face. Already shy, Affleck had to contend with being considered average in the classroom and less than spectacular in looks, but if he wanted to establish a career in anything, he had to surmount the hardships. He possessed one valuable tool lacking in many others—a passion for something, in his case acting.

"We're Going to Take the Town by Storm!"

Affleck had the assistance of another person at Cambridge Rindge and Latin School besides Matt Damon. Drama teacher Gerry Speca not only cultivated Affleck's love of acting, but took the raw talent and added a key missing ingredient—discipline. He explained to his pupil that talent without direction produces little of value. To succeed one needed to add responsibility and discipline to natural skills.

Affleck and Damon followed Speca's advice, at least as far as acting was concerned. The pair frequently discussed their dreams for the future. Most every lunch hour at school, the two could be found in the cafeteria, sitting alone at a table with partially devoured lunches, chatting about what would happen to them once they headed west to Hollywood. Other students scoffed at their dreams, for as Affleck confided to a magazine reporter, "I

An Educator's Gift

As a high school student, Ben Affleck benefited from learning from a demanding teacher. Gerry Speca, the drama teacher, expected his students to excel and thus set high standards for the class. In return he promised to give his students 100 percent of his effort, and he delivered on his promise. Speca helped the students write plays or read lines with them. As a result of his tutorage, both Ben Affleck and Matt Damon joined a Boston acting group that won a prestigious youth drama award from the local newspaper.

Affleck explained that Speca's greatest asset was that he showed students how to be organized and how to take responsibility for their actions. He expected students to be proud if they performed well or handed in a stellar play, but he demanded they accept blame for any shortcomings instead of shifting the fault to someone else. Few weeks go by that Affleck and Damon do not think of their teacher.

guess you could say we were theater nerds, which certainly wasn't as cool as playing on the basketball team."[16]

The criticism failed to deter the two, however. Damon and Affleck avidly pursued their plans, ignoring any taunts that might have arisen from students eating at nearby tables. "We'd sit there with our trays and these crappy little 50-cent sandwiches," Affleck told the *Boston Phoenix*, "and we'd say things like, 'We're going to be big actors! We're going to take the town [Hollywood] by storm!'"[17]

They may have boasted of dreams so immense that they sometimes did not even believe themselves, but in the process they planted the seeds for success. Affleck admits, "In high school, our friendship got more intense as we realized how much we both had similar goals. We had these fantasies about all the things we were going to do, and they were all sort of silly and romantic and half-baked. We never really imagined that any of them would come true."[18] Yet, whether or not they realized it, those seemingly futile lunch exercises molded and hardened the still-emerging desires to make it big.

"I Would Really, Really Appreciate It"

The cafeteria sessions ended after Affleck's sophomore year when the older Damon headed off to college. Although he did not have to travel far—he attended nearby Harvard—his departure left Affleck on his own at high school. Affleck still had the close-knit group of neighborhood friends, which included his younger brother, Casey, but most did not share Affleck's aspirations.

The two still met after classes to discuss their plans, the books they had read, or what they observed. Affleck's perspective toward Cambridge's illustrious universities began to change. He, Damon, and the other neighborhood buddies in their tight clan had always sensed a difference between themselves, the "townies," and the college "imports" who attended Harvard and MIT. They resented what they perceived as Harvard arrogance toward the homebred youth. That changed once Damon entered Harvard, intermingled with these students, and found that, rather than being different, they shared many common traits. Affleck realized the same as he more frequently stepped onto Harvard's campus.

"There were the real townie kids and there were these university kids at MIT and Harvard," he told a magazine reporter. "It was weird when Matt got into Harvard and was able to see both sides of it. I would go hang out with him there and we had all these prejudices about these Harvard kids. Then I kind of got to know a lot of them and they were really interesting, kind of cool people."[19] He had learned a valuable lesson about the dangers of judging people before you know something about them. The point would later be made in some of Affleck's films.

Affleck continued to act in a handful of television commercials while he finished high school. As always, his mother insisted that her son lead as normal a life as possible, a philosophy glaringly illustrated with Affleck's first automobile. While other students zoomed around town in late-model cars, Affleck purchased a four-door 1977 Toyota Corona station wagon. The eleven-year-old car sported rust patches and leaked water into the interior so badly that in winter the puddles froze on the floorboard, but at least he had a vehicle. Every time Affleck climbed into the car, praying the engine would respond, he used it as motivation to work hard for something better.

"It just sucked. But I had a car and I got around. I was always so envious of the guys with the Lexus and Mercedes and the big SUV. They're always middle-aged guys. I said, 'This is wasted on this guy, this is unfair, he doesn't appreciate this car and I would really, really appreciate it.'"[20]

One day he would have that glamorous car, he told himself. Before he could reach that point, though, he had to establish his acting career.

Early Lessons

Affleck's acting career gained momentum during his high school years. He continued to travel to New York to film commercials, but he now added more feature films and television work to his résumé. In 1987 he won the role of Billy Hearn in another made-for-television miniseries, *Hands of a Stranger*. The film gave him not only more exposure but the opportunity to act with two noted professionals, Armand Assante and Blair Brown. Affleck studied the mannerisms and habits of his successful costars to see how he might become a more rounded actor.

In 1987 Affleck worked alongside accomplished actor Armand Assante in the television miniseries Hands of a Stranger.

Affleck gained much valuable experience in 1987 when he landed the lead role in a film about Eskimos called *Atuk*. Excited to have his first leading role to his credit, Affleck busily prepared for the film's shooting, sure that this would be a stepping-stone to greater things. Before filming ended, however, the production company experienced problems in financing and shut down. A brokenhearted Affleck, in effect fired along with every other actor on the set, learned a hard but valuable lesson about the unpredictability of the movie industry and the lack of control an actor often has over the course of a movie.

"I don't know that any actor feels secure,"[21] he stated about the disappointing result of *Atuk*. At least Affleck learned very early in his career that the acting business can be cruel, that one can be dismissed at any time. He realized that he could not count on anything as certain until the final touches had been added and the film was showing on theater screens.

Early Obstacles

At the same time, Affleck faced another obstacle to his film career. His parents, perhaps seeing the future more clearly than their star-struck teenage son, tried to point out the pitfalls of Hollywood. They explained that of the thousands of hopefuls each year who try to break into the entertainment industry, only a small handful succeed. The rest, they told him, exist on rejection, shattered dreams, and sparse meals. Neither wanted their son to face a seemingly endless string of disappointments.

Matt Damon joked of Ben's mother, Chris, that "every time we sat down to dinner, Chris would say, 'Why don't you guys become doctors?'"[22] It was not so much that the parents wanted to talk the boys out of their dreams. They wanted to make sure they investigated every possible angle and understood what they faced before leaping into the frenzy.

"I think our parents were concerned because everybody knows that acting is a difficult career," says Affleck:

> I don't think they were that happy with the prospect of their kids facing a lifetime of rejection and scraping by for a sandwich and hoping we'd get free refills at the age of forty-five. But Matt and I were very straightforward about wanting to be actors. I really think that everybody would like to be an actor. Why wouldn't they? It's great work if you can get it. The one thing that prevents most people from saying, "I'm just gonna go to Hollywood!" is that it seems unrealistic.[23]

The parents had discharged their responsibility to point out the dangers as well as the rewards of a film career. Affleck, with friend Damon in tow, showed that he was willing to take a step from which so many others shrank—he decided to go to Hollywood. His parents eased off when they saw his determined reaction and realized the acting bug was not just a phase through which their son was passing, but they had not yet been completely convinced that the path their son had selected was the proper one. In the meantime, to be safe, Chris Affleck put most of her son's money into a trust fund to pay for college tuition.

"I Had to Be the Man of the House"

Affleck's mother had another reason to worry about the security of her son—she had to be the sole guardian of the family's welfare. Her husband, Timothy, perhaps unhappy that he failed to find a stable job, started to drink heavily before Ben entered high school. The situation placed an incredible strain on things at home. Ben never knew if he would walk into a calm setting or whether his parents would be fighting. During turbulent times, Ben attempted to play the role of peacemaker and convince his parents to stop arguing, but the young boy was not capable of solving their problems.

The drinking reached a critical stage and so disrupted the family that in 1984 Chris and Timothy decided divorce would be best for all. While Chris remained in Cambridge with Ben and Casey, Tim Affleck returned to California, where in 1990 he finally entered the ABC Club rehabilitation center in Indio and stopped drinking.

In the absence of his father, Ben Affleck felt a responsibility to be the man of the house for his mother and the father-figure for younger brother, Casey. This placed a heavy burden on the teenager, who would have preferred focusing on baseball and video games.

Affleck explained the effects of the drinking and divorce in a later magazine interview: "I had to be the man of the house. I had to take more responsibility at an earlier age. I think it left me kind of schizophrenic—I never knew if I was young or old. I can be serious and heavy and feel very burdened and adult. Alternately, I can be very juvenile."[24] These two sides of his personality, reflecting both maturity and immaturity, would be apparent in years to come.

Ben Affleck saw almost nothing of his father throughout his high school years. Not until he headed west to start his acting career did the two reestablish a relationship. By then, Affleck had already abandoned plans to earn a college degree.

Acting over Study

After graduating from high school in 1990, Affleck followed his mother's wishes and enrolled at the University of Vermont. The

Ben's Little Brother

Casey Affleck, Ben's younger brother and the person Ben says is the closest to him, was born August 12, 1975, in Massachusetts. After attending Columbia University, where he majored in physics, Casey followed his big brother into the film industry.

He first acted in television films. In 1987 he starred in *Lemon Sky*, three years before playing a young Robert F. Kennedy in the miniseries *The Kennedys of Massachusetts*. In addition to his role in *Good Will Hunting*,

Casey has appeared in a number of major projects, including *To Die For* with Nicole Kidman, *Chasing Amy*, *American Pie 2*, and *Ocean's Eleven*.

Casey has learned from observing his brother's career. He stated that because of the difficulties Ben has experienced with the press, Casey has been more guarded in what he tells the media.

Ben shares a very close relationship with his younger brother Casey, who is also an actor.

fact that a high school girlfriend studied there made his decision easier, but Affleck was not committed to college. He continued his education almost as an afterthought, as something to do because his family wanted him to and because some of his friends did that. Deep down, though, he could not see a reason for poring over volumes of useless facts when all he wanted was to star in movies.

He tolerated only one semester at Vermont. The allure of California, and in particular Hollywood, proved too potent. After promising his mother that he would seriously hit the books, the eighteen-year-old Affleck transferred to Occidental College in Eagle Rock, California, in 1991, ostensibly to study Middle Eastern culture and history.

Affleck had little intention of pursuing a college degree, however. In fact, he spent more time reconnecting with his father, who had by now quit drinking. The two enjoyed long discussions about the past, about his father's addiction, and what Affleck hoped to achieve with his life. Affleck may not have gained much from college, but he strengthened a bond with his father that had been severely damaged.

He was as disinterested in Occidental as he had been in Vermont, and before the first year ended, he had dropped out of that institution as well. College classes, in his opinion, simply wasted time and stood in the way of what he really wanted. He had the talent and intelligence to excel at Occidental; he lacked the discipline and the interest. He wanted to move on to what he considered his life's work.

"I'm somebody who doesn't like to do something unless I can really commit to it. I could do neither one [school and acting] well. And so I finally left school and pursued [acting] full time."[25]

Affleck left Occidental and started on the path taken by thousands of other Hollywood hopefuls. Like the men and women before him, Affleck would quickly discover numerous obstacles on the road to the top.

Chapter 3

"There's a Side of You That People Really Haven't Seen"

PARENTS ARGUE WITH their growing sons and daughters over all sorts of issues. Dads might not approve of the boy their daughter brought home, moms look askance at their sons' dirty fingernails and tattered T-shirts. Ben Affleck and his mother were no different, except their disagreements centered largely over college and Ben's desire to act. Ben wanted to put full effort into building an entertainment career, while his mother contended that a college degree would create a safety net for her son in case he did not make it in Hollywood. She supported his dreams, but thought he should be more cautious in pursuing them. Affleck chose a more aggressive approach.

In an effort to emphasize her point, Affleck's mother arranged a dinner meeting between her son and a man who had been trying to break into acting for two decades. Throughout the meal he spoke to Affleck about the hazards of acting, and explained that he had earned the paltry sum of eight thousand dollars through acting, an average of only four hundred dollars a year. This blatant attempt to illustrate the difficulties of the acting profession made little impression on Affleck, but he would soon learn firsthand just how difficult the entertainment business can be.

A Rocky Start

After arriving in Hollywood, Affleck discovered that even minor parts were hard to obtain, and the competition at auditions was fierce. He drifted from one obscure acting job to another, none of which paid much, and found it difficult to break out from independent films made on a shoestring into bigger-budget productions made by established studios.

At least he had the company of his closest friend, Matt Damon, who had joined him in California to establish his own acting career. The two lived in a number of rundown Los Angeles apartments, sometimes with other acting hopefuls, pooled their money to buy meals and pay bills, and took turns sleeping on the bed or on the couch. They were a long way away from the glitz and glamour that permeated the city.

Affleck claims that he was "barely able to pay the $300 a month for a one-bedroom hole"[26] in which he lived. He once argued with a roommate over who got to keep the less than two dollars in change they both claimed they found in the couch because each wanted to purchase a $1.29 chicken dinner special at

Aspiring actors line up to audition for a part on a soap opera. Once in Hollywood, Affleck faced fierce competition at auditions and found parts hard to obtain.

In 1991 Affleck earned twenty thousand dollars for his role in the television movie Danielle Steele's Daddy, *which starred Lynda Carter and Patrick Duffy (pictured).*

a local restaurant. The dilapidated Los Angeles neighborhood made his middle-class Cambridge home street look affluent, and he told friends, with more than a touch of concern in his voice, that he saw more drugs sold in one day in his new neighborhood than he had in his entire life up to that point.

Despite his less-than-ideal living conditions, Affleck forged ahead in Hollywood, slowly assembling a portfolio of performances. In October 1991 he portrayed an eighteen-year-old youth who fathers a child in the made-for-television movie *Danielle Steele's Daddy*. Affleck garnered praise for the part, especially for his work during a seven-minute segment in which he pled before a judge for custody of the child. Affleck's moving entreaty showed he possessed the ability to put emotion into his acting.

Affleck earned twenty thousand dollars for the part, a lordly sum for the struggling actor. He enjoyed the opportunity to work with veteran actors Patrick Duffy and Lynda Carter, best known for playing Wonder Woman on television. An excited Affleck could hardly wait to cash the check, but his friends were only interested in knowing whether he developed a relationship with Lynda Carter.

The Fear of Failure

The few high points of his early career failed to neutralize the many lows. Affleck believed he had what it took to succeed, but he could not seem to convince other people in the industry, some of whom scoffed that he lacked the proper "look" to be a star. "Agents used to tell me, 'You have baby fat on your face,' and 'You're not good-looking enough,'" said Affleck. "For a long time the thing was blond and waifish, and that's not my thing. I was always getting characterized as 'beefy.' That's just not a flattering thing to say about anybody."[27]

Producers dismissed Affleck for his six foot, three inch stature, a height considered too tall for leading man roles. He faced the same obstacles that deterred hundreds of other actors from attaining their goals, but as he had done with high school critics and his parents, he dug deep into a reservoir of inner strength and decided to gut it out:

> That fear [of failure] stays with you so intensely and you're constantly just getting turned down for what you think of as the most vapid, stupid kind of paycheck, *Baywatch* things, and you think, if I'm not good enough for this then I'm not going to make it. This town is too hard, and people were always telling me, "You're too big, you're too tall, you can only play bullies and you will never be a leading man."[28]

When Affleck felt the world was stacked against him, he at least could now turn to the father he had not seen in so long. Since Timothy Affleck lived only a few hours away in an isolated desert town in California, Ben frequently visited his father. There, in the withering heat, the two would sit and talk in the small, peaceful town that seemed lifted from the 1950s. Ben found that he was talking to the one man who, because he battled his own demons, could empathize with the struggling actor.

A Modest Start

Things took a more advantageous turn in 1992 when Affleck appeared in a movie called *School Ties*. The film, which took a serious look at the issue of anti-Semitism among high school students, gained decent reviews for its principal actors, among whom were

Affleck, Matt Damon, Brendan Fraser (who later starred in *The Mummy*), and Chris O'Donnell (Robin in two of the *Batman* movies). Affleck and Damon played two bigoted wealthy students who target a Jewish student, portrayed by Fraser, for abuse.

When the careers of Fraser and O'Donnell received huge boosts from the film and Affleck's continued to stumble, he wondered if he would ever break out of the pack. It seemed that Affleck saw the same group of young actors auditioning for the same roles, and that he received a script only if one of his competitors had already considered and passed on it. He plodded on, however, hoping for the big role that had so far eluded him.

Until then, he had to console himself with the thiry-five thousand dollars he received for his work in *School Ties*. He and Damon, who earned the same amount, suddenly thought they had struck it rich, rented a more spacious house on the beach, and invited all their friends to visit. For a brief time life was a party for the fortunate duo, but the good times quickly ended. First of all, they learned that the government expected fifteen thousand dollars in taxes, and they quickly realized how fast a group of friends could go through the remainder.

When Affleck and Damon ran out of money, they had to give up their home on the beach and return to more affordable, meaning smaller and dingier, apartments. Affleck lived in so many different places that he must have felt he belonged with a nomadic tribe—he occupied apartments in Glendale, Eagle Rock, Hollywood, West Hollywood, Venice, among other spots. Finally, in a move that restored stability, he and Damon rented a place near the Hollywood Bowl with a few of their high school friends. Roots had always meant a great deal to Affleck, and if he could not establish a film career while living in Cambridge, the next best thing was to bring Cambridge to him.

The buddies from high school certainly treated him with more respect than Hollywood producers, and apparently more respect than the girls whose interest he failed to attract. He explained in a magazine interview that he was turned down for dates with alarming frequency during this period. The one serious relationship he enjoyed in the early 1990s ended when the girl cheated on him, an action that so humiliated Affleck that he had difficulty talking about it.

School Ties, the Launching Pad to Stardom

In 1992 Ben Affleck starred in the film *School Ties*. Set in a 1950s New England preparatory school, the movie tackles the heated issue of discrimination against a Jewish student.

What made the movie particularly notable was the large number of young male actors who subsequently built stellar film careers, in part because of their work in *School Ties*. In addition to Affleck, the movie showcased the talents of Matt Damon, who went on to make *The Rainmaker* and *Saving Private Ryan* among other films; Brendan Fraser, who starred in *The Mummy*, *The Mummy Returns*, and *The Quiet American;* Cole Hauser, who appeared in *Dazed and Confused*, *Good Will Hunting*, *Hart's War*, and *2 Fast 2 Furious;* and Chris O'Donnell, who moved on to *Scent of a Woman*, *The Three Musketeers*, *Circle of Friends*, 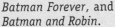 *Batman Forever*, and *Batman and Robin*.

School Ties retains a good reputation, both for its quality and its cast.

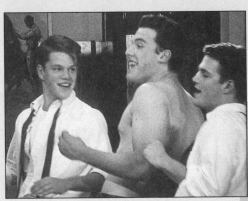

School Ties *featured a young and talented cast, including (from left to right) Damon, Affleck, and Chris O'Donnell.*

"He Is So Not That"

In his eagerness to gain more exposure, Affleck may have erred in selecting his next role. *Dazed and Confused,* a 1993 comedy about the final day of high school for a group of Texas teenagers, presented an appealing topic, but it placed Affleck into the type of role from which he had difficulty escaping in the future. Producers asked him to play a bully in a cast of otherwise likable characters, a device that set him apart from the rest and made him more likely to be asked for similar type roles in subsequent films. If Affleck were to break out of the pack and establish a top-notch acting career, he had to prove he could play a variety of parts instead of being typecast as a heavy.

Matthew McConaughey, who played one of the movie's more appealing characters, moved on to star in *A Time to Kill,* but Affleck was offered nothing but similar roles—minor characters that gained the audience's animosity. "After I had done *Dazed and Confused,* where I was the only unlikable character in a cast full of likable characters, everybody [in Hollywood production circles] thought I was a [jerk], which is not much help when you're looking for a job," explained Affleck in a magazine interview. "After that movie I was probably the poorest I ever was."[29]

Affleck followed that mishap with another bomb when he played a Texas high school football quarterback in the television series *Against the Grain,* which aired on NBC. When the program failed to draw a decent audience, the network quickly canceled it and once again Affleck was hustling to auditions.

The next few years proved difficult for Affleck, as he attempted to win that one role that could show his talent as an actor. He admitted that he battled despair during these times, sometimes wondering if the constant auditions and subsisting on canned food

Affleck played a high school quarterback in the short-lived NBC television series Against the Grain.

was worth it, and stated that he was "one or two *Family Matters* episodes away from flipping burgers."[30]

The turning point in Affleck's career came in 1995 when he captured a key role in the film *Mallrats*. The role, as one of a group of teenagers hanging out at a local mall, was not as significant as was his association with director Kevin Smith. Affleck knew that Smith had previously made a movie for only twenty-seven thousand dollars and, hopeful of one day making his own films, wanted to observe how the filmmaker could complete a project on such a small budget.

Smith had his eye on Affleck as well. He thought other producers and directors had miscast the struggling actor and believed that Affleck could do far more than play a rough guy. Smith told *Premier* magazine, "I was like, 'Why is Affleck always playing the bully? He is so not that. Around that time I started writing *Chasing Amy* and I decided to write him a leading-man part."[31]

The incident illustrates one key to success—dogged pursuit of a dream, despite hazards. An unexpected break can come from the least likely source. In this case, without realizing it Affleck had drawn the notice of a director who would play a prominent role in his life over the next few years.

"The Theater Was Packed"

While he was making the movie *Mallrats*, Kevin Smith also wrote the script for *Chasing Amy*. Attracted by Affleck's potential, Smith included a key part especially for him, a part that leaned on what he saw as Affleck's tender, sweeter nature. He ignored the advice of another producer who scoffed at his intent to use Affleck, who, the producer claimed, was too tall to be a leading man. When Smith informed Affleck what he was doing, he added, "I think there's a side of you that people really haven't seen. You can really be a leading man and do some romantic things."[32]

An astonished Affleck could hardly believe what he heard. For so long he had labored to escape the label of the heavy, of playing roles that drew nothing but animosity from audiences, and now that goal seemed at hand. He readily agreed to star in the film. Affleck followed *Chasing Amy* with another tender performance in *Going All the Way*, a film about a former high school football star who returns home from fighting in the Korean War.

Mallrats

By acting in the 1996 film *Mallrats*, Affleck found more than just another opportunity to perform. He also came into contact with a director who would later help him sell the script of *Good Will Hunting*, Kevin Smith.

In *Mallrats*, Smith, known for making cutting-edge movies that appealed to a younger audience, told the story of two friends, Brodie Bruce and T.S. Quint, who are both dumped by their girlfriends on the same day. In an effort to forget their misery, the two head to the local mall, where they encounter a strange array of characters, including Jay and Silent Bob, two characters from an earlier Smith film called *Clerks*. After realizing they cannot live without their girls, the pair decides to try to win them back by creating a scene at the mall.

Though it has gained a cult following, *Mallrats* was special to Affleck's career in that it placed him and Smith together. Smith's timely assistance mere days before a deadline ensured that Affleck and Damon retained the rights to the script of *Good Will Hunting*.

In addition to Affleck, *Mallrats* starred Jason Lee and Shannen Doherty. Director Kevin Smith played a small part, as did legendary comic book writer, Stan Lee, cocreator of characters such as Spiderman and Daredevil.

The two vehicles appeared in theaters in 1997 and both were accepted for screening at Robert Redford's prestigious Sundance Film Festival in Park City, Utah.

For the first time in his career, Affleck enjoyed flattering reviews for his ability to portray flawed, emotional characters. His work in the two films impressed studio executives, who began noticing the full range of Affleck's talents.

Affleck could barely contain his elation and surprise. He mentioned to *Biography* magazine in 2000 that "Everyone was saying there's really good buzz [about both films]. I sort of brushed it off. I was thinking, 'How can there be buzz, no one has seen the movie.' Then I went to that screening [for *Going All the Way*]. The theater was packed, and there was everybody that you read about. It was astonishing."[33]

One man he met at the festival later interviewed him for a lengthy magazine article. Writer Bernard Weinraub encountered Affleck at the brink of Affleck's breakthrough, just as Affleck's name was about to rocket to the top of the Hollywood film industry's roster of stars. An impressed Weinraub, more accustomed to working with arrogant individuals who had an agenda to promote, walked away with a favorable impression of the youthful actor:

> The first time I met Ben was at a Miramax [studio] party at the Sundance Film Festival. . . . It was the year that *Going All the Way* was shown at the festival, and Affleck was practically unknown. He seemed to be the tallest guy in the room, and he was also one of the most engaging. When he heard that I had once covered politics he dropped all the conversation about acting and wanted to talk about President [Bill] Clinton and his troubles with Congress. He seemed not only smart but surprisingly well versed in politics.[34]

After years of struggling, Ben Affleck was about to take a gigantic step upward. With the pair of 1997 films, *Chasing Amy* and

Kevin Smith directs Affleck in a scene from Chasing Amy. *Impressed with Affleck's strong performance, critics gave the film glowing reviews.*

Going All the Way, he had shattered the mold in which producers had confined him as only being able to play tough-guy parts. Affleck would later count 1997 as the key year of his life, in part because of those two films. However, the year marked a watershed in Affleck's life not so much for those movies as for his next 1997 project, a film that brought Oscar calling.

Chapter 4

"We'd Just Make This Movie Ourselves"

I<small>N THE LATTER</small> half of 1997, Ben Affleck made his dreams of success and stardom a reality, after years of hard work, sacrifice, and worry. Through all those years, Affleck maintained a steady course even when things looked bleak, and because of that persistence, he triumphed. The fact that he accomplished it with his best friend, Matt Damon, made the journey sweeter.

"This Is Really Good"

Coming fast on the success of *Chasing Amy* and *Going All the Way*, Affleck's third film of the year brought widespread acclaim to the actor and forever altered his life. The movie originated a few years earlier from one of Matt Damon's college papers, a scene he had written for a Harvard playwriting class taught by David Wheeler. The brief story, about a young man named Will Hunting, impressed Damon's fellow students, and Damon liked the idea enough that he dreamed one day it might become something bigger.

"It occurred to me that this guy, this Will Hunting, could have big screen potential," explained Damon. "Hey, I wanted to play him! But then I thought, 'You're dreaming, man.'"[35]

Damon decided to share his thoughts with Affleck when the actor returned to Boston for the 1992 Christmas holidays. Affleck read the script, then agreed to act out the scene with Damon in his Harvard class. Though the pair enjoyed an enthusiastic reaction from the college class and from an assortment of professors in attendance, they at first had little idea what to do with the script.

The two discussed possible notions of doing something with the writing, but quickly returned to their various careers. Affleck headed back to Los Angeles and another round of auditions, while Damon resumed his class load at Harvard.

During spring break of 1993, Damon traveled to Los Angeles to audition for a role he eventually received in the movie *Geronimo*. While there he again showed the scene, now up to forty pages, to Affleck. After reading it, an impressed Affleck turned to his friend and said, "This is really good. We should write this together."[36]

So Much Energy and Passion

Although Damon had written the entire forty-page script, he readily agreed to let his friend help flesh it out. Affleck may not have lasted long in college, but everyone who knew him realized that beneath the surface lurked a keen intelligence. Growing up in Cambridge, the two liked to proclaim that Matt was the serious student and Ben was the clown, but that was no more than friendly banter. "Ben's too modest to tell you this," stated Damon

The Origins of a Script

In the fall of 1992, Matt Damon enrolled in a Harvard creative writing class taught by Anthony Kubiak. One of the course requirements was writing a short story, something Damon had never seriously attempted. After kicking around a few ideas, Damon decided to pen a tale about characters he knew well—the residents of Cambridge.

As Chris Nickson relates in *Matt Damon: An Unauthorized Biography*, Damon did not have high expectations for the story that later earned Ben Affleck and him so much acclaim: "I handed it in and it didn't really go anywhere, but it had a couple of these characters. [Kubiak] told me I should keep writing it. I kept telling him that I couldn't end it, but he would say it was a full-length [piece] and [that I] should write it into a full-length piece. So he really encouraged me to do it."

Damon took the revamped story into his Harvard drama class, where he and Affleck later acted out a scene. From that point on, *Good Will Hunting* occupied a major part of both Affleck's and Damon's lives.

to a reporter, "but he's the most well-read person I know. He's certainly a lot smarter than I am."[37] Damon welcomed Affleck's assistance in transforming a half-formed thought into something marketable.

They labored on and off for the next few months, as both had other work that demanded their attention. During that time, though, the story plot simmered in their minds. Every time one or the other returned from a failed audition or learned that a part they desired had been given to another young actor, the story assumed greater significance. This could be their ticket out of Hollywood's entrance level; this could jettison them from the stream of disappointments and from their lives in shabby apartments.

Finally, a potent combination of frustration over the inability to find work and the desire to make something of the script prompted Affleck and Damon to take the unusual step that led them ultimately to a Los Angeles stage, with both clutching an Oscar statuette. They decided that since producers were not knocking down their door with tempting offers, they would go ahead and write roles for themselves. They would not crumble; they would take the initiative.

"If no one else was going to give us the chance to do the kind of acting we thought we could do," said Affleck, "we decided we'd just make this movie ourselves—however we could do it, low-budget, whatever."[38]

Damon could not agree more with Affleck. They had endured school taunts while they sat at cafeteria tables plotting their dreams, and if Hollywood was not about to offer them their chance, they would create their own. "We wrote it out of frustration," said Damon. "It was like, 'Why are we sitting here? Let's make our own movie. And if people come to see it, they come; and if they don't, they don't. Either way, it beats sitting here going crazy.' When you have so much energy and so much passion for it and nobody cares, it's just the worst feeling."[39]

Living in Hollywood, Affleck and Damon saw numerous examples of failures, but they ignored them in favor of one that triumphed—the 1976 Oscar-winning film *Rocky*. Its writer, Sylvester Stallone, had finally brought his script to the big screen

Sylvester Stallone wrote and starred in the Oscar-winning Rocky *(pictured). His success inspired Affleck and Damon to bring their script for* Good Will Hunting *to the big screen.*

after years of pushing and prodding top film executives. He often defied their demands and met with their disapproval because he insisted on writing and making the movie according to his vision, and he ultimately succeeded. Affleck and Damon believed that if one person could do it, so could they.

A Script Is Born

The two started serious work on the script in late 1993 and into 1994. Ben slept on the couch in Matt's apartment while they devoted full time to fleshing out the script. As the better typist, Ben sat at the keyboard as the words flowed between the pair.

When work on other films placed them in different parts of the country, Affleck and Damon faxed pages of revisions to each other. When together, they acted out their words and improvised new lines as they slowly breathed life into the tale. It helped that they had each other, for neither had studied screenwriting and neither had a formula to follow. Instead, they trusted each other's abilities and relied on the fact that they knew each other so well and shared so many experiences together.

Affleck explained how their familiarity with each other helped the writing process, "He'll [Matt] say something like, 'Remember that time? Glass-eyed Leslie?' And I'll say, 'Yeah, yeah, at

Little-Known Facts About *Good Will Hunting*

While many movie fans have seen Ben Affleck's *Good Will Hunting* and know the story that appeared on-screen, many behind-the-scenes pieces of information have not been circulated, most having to do with the senses of humor exhibited by Affleck, Damon, and the rest of the cast. In their 1998 biography *Matt Damon: A Biography*, Maxine Diamond and Harriet Hemmings include the following material:

1) The two playwrights had fun creating certain character names. The first name of the college professor who tries to draw Will Hunting into the mathematical world is Gerry, while his student assistant's first name is Tom. That was a humorous take-off on the famous cartoon cat and mouse duo, Tom and Jerry.

2) In one scene, Robin Williams talks to Damon's character, Will Hunting, about his deceased wife's odd tendency to pass gas. Both Williams and Damon laugh uncontrollably during the scene, mainly because neither knew that Williams was going to say those words. The script called for Williams to discuss his wife's habit of turning off the alarm clock at night, thereby making Williams's character late for work, but Williams saw an opportunity to improvise. Damon freely went along with the improvisation, which formed a moving portion of the film.

3) In another scene, Will Hunting spots a painting in the psychologist's office and criticizes it for being amateurish. More humor existed in that scene than is obvious—the painting was one of director Gus Van Sant's creations.

4) In spite of the humor, no one made fun of the film when the receipts tumbled in. It quickly rose to the top of Miramax's list of films, passing the previous champion moneymaker, *Pulp Fiction*.

Affleck and Damon incorporated subtle humor into their Good Will Hunting *script.*

McDonald's! Glass-eyed Leslie. Let's use that!' It's a kind of familiarity that gives you a certain shorthand. We have a common sense of humor. The most reassuring thing is that you can look at it and think, 'This is better than if we did this by ourselves.'"[40]

They also trusted their minds and hearts to lead them down the right path. Often, they simply asked each other whether dialogue they had just written would be fun to act. If they decided not, out went the part and another revision started. Common sense, creativity, instinct, and talent carried them along as the pages mounted.

Even when driving in the same car, one would recite new lines while the other took a notebook out of the glove compartment and jotted hurried notes that would later be turned into another page of the script.

"[The script] went off in all directions, and some of the things we came up with just wound up in the garbage," claims Damon. "But some were great and we built on them."[41] Characters experienced transformations and settings changed. The script mushroomed into more than one thousand pages, nearly ten times longer than the average Hollywood script, and the two formed an understanding that Damon would play the lead role of Will Hunting while Affleck would automatically receive the main part in their second effort.

"And the Offers Kept Going Up"

By November 1994 the pair had shortened their still-lengthy script and taken it to Matt's agent, who agreed to pitch it to the major producers in hopes of whetting their interest in the material. At that point the project seemed to take on a life of its own; four heady days later Affleck and Damon signed a deal with Castle Rock Entertainment.

The action kicked off on a Monday. An offer of fifteen thousand dollars quickly tumbled in, producing a stunned reaction from Affleck and Damon. "When the phone started ringing, we were ready to take the first offer, which was $15,000,"[42] Affleck says, but their agent persuaded them to wait. He had seen bidding wars before and correctly concluded that a larger offer was on the horizon. All they needed was a little patience.

The two, drooling over the initial offer and eager to get their hands on some money, listened to the more experienced agent.

It was difficult, for both still occupied a sparse apartment and lived frugally. In fact, inaccurate rumors later spread that at the time they sold their script, Affleck was homeless. Those accounts, while embellishing the tale into something near legend status, were far from the truth. He slept on Damon's couch, but Affleck had not plummeted so far down as to have no residence.

They did not have to wait long for good news. In four hectic days that left Affleck and Damon practically speechless, offers poured into the agent's office. By Thursday evening, an agreement had been written, discussed among all the major principals, and signed. "It was wild," stated an exuberant Affleck after the whirlwind week. "We were kind of giddy. We would come out of a meeting with both our heads to the phone waiting to hear the newest offer. And the offers kept going up."[43]

The two felt a powerful mixture of emotions at this critical time in their lives. After years of struggling, of ignoring detractors, and listening to their parents' objections, Affleck and Damon had arrived at the precise moment for which they had so long labored. They felt like they had won the lottery, but also worried that the turn of events would alter them in drastic ways. "We were talking about the difference between eating Spam every day and being able to buy a three-bedroom house with a pool table and new cars,"[44] said Matt Damon. Would they remain the same guys that had emerged from the working-class section of Cambridge?

Castle Rock, a company with an impressive record of high-quality films, outbid the other firms with an offer of $600,000. Even after taxes and agent fees, Affleck and Damon each took home $130,000, a princely sum after years of struggle. "I kept telling Matt to pinch me," explained Affleck. "I thought, 'It couldn't be this easy!'"[45]

Family and friends in Massachusetts shared their happiness, not because they had pocketed a tidy sum, but because they had moved much closer to realizing their dream of establishing a stellar reputation in the entertainment field.

A Revised Script

The initial glow of success did not last long. Castle Rock agreed to finance the film but demanded that drastic changes be made to the lengthy script. Castle Rock executive and longtime actor and director Rob Reiner explained that the script contained too much action. Instead, he wanted Affleck and Damon to focus more on character development. Reiner suggested that they eliminate certain portions, which had Will Hunting involved with the Federal Bureau of Investigation (FBI) and with the National Aeronautic and Space Agency (NASA), and place more emphasis on Hunting's struggle to define himself.

Affleck and Damon had mistakenly assumed that the movie needed an antagonist as a rival for Hunting. Reiner helped them understand that they did not need that element, as long as they created an internal struggle in their main character. Will Hunting versus the forces of evil, whether represented by a villainous character or by a dastardly organization, would be fine, but Will Hunting battling his own demons could create a far more powerful film.

The two immediately started revising the script. Out went the FBI and NASA—although the Central Intelligence Agency occupied a small portion of the final product—and in came a psychologist and a girlfriend. They met with esteemed author William Goldman, who had won screenplay Oscars in 1970 for *Butch*

The Selling of a Script

The four hectic November days during which Ben Affleck and Matt Damon sold their script to Castle Rock proved unnerving in more ways than one. When the phone immediately started ringing with offers the pair, weary of living off cheap food, yelled to their agent that he should accept one of them, but the agent reminded them they had to be more patient.

That was difficult, since Affleck and Damon eagerly imagined better times ahead and wanted them to start as soon as possible. The phone rang again, but one of their roommates beat them to the receiver. As Damon recalled in Chris Nickson's *Matt Damon: An Unauthorized Biography*, "It was for my roommate, and it was this girl he had dated in college, and my roommate was, like, 'Hey, how are you?' And we [Affleck and Damon] were, like, '*Hang* the phone up!' He was really bummed because they hadn't talked in three years."

Four days later they were ecstatic they had listened to their agent instead of their stomachs. Castle Rock's offer set them on a wild course leading to fame and stardom.

Director Rob Reiner advised Affleck and Damon to eliminate many of their script's action scenes and focus instead on character development.

Cassidy and the Sundance Kid and in 1977 for *All the President's Men*, and incorporated some of his suggestions. By the time they had completed their revisions, less than one hundred pages of the original script remained.

The basic story now centered on a disturbed young man, Will Hunting, growing up in the same tough Cambridge neighborhoods in which Affleck had matured. Instead of attending college, despite being a mathematical genius, Hunting takes a position as janitor at Harvard University, similar to the occupation once held by Timothy Affleck. Throughout the film, Hunting tries to work through the anger he carries over being physically abused as a child and finds himself pulled in many directions. A brilliant Harvard professor spots him solving an elaborate mathematical problem that had eluded the talents of his best students, finds out who Hunting is, and pressures him to join his university program; a girlfriend offers love and sympathy while seeking his devotion in return; his childhood friends, a group remarkably similar to Affleck's and Damon's Cambridge buddies, provide a safe, yet unchallenging, environment.

Hunting's quandary centers on his struggle to mature into a responsible, caring man while facing the turbulence in his life. With the help of a psychologist, Hunting comes to terms with his past, realizes he is not at fault for the abuse he suffered, and simultaneously helps the psychologist accept and move on from his wife's untimely death.

The script was finally ready for filming. Affleck and Damon expected Castle Rock to take it from there and start filming any day, but, the movie studio unexpectedly dropped a series of obstacles in their path. Affleck and Damon had not yet reached their pinnacle.

Chapter 5

"You Guys Really Did It"

AT THE PRECISE moment when the two should have been jumping for joy, frustration and exasperation set in instead. For months the script lay undeveloped in Castle Rock offices, mainly because of creative differences between the studio and the authors. What had seemed a dream come true almost ended in a nightmare, as Affleck and Damon searched for a way to bring their story to the big screen. Determined to maintain control over what they considered their creation, the two had negotiated a certain amount of control over the film, confident any issues that came up could be worked out. Now Castle Rock was resisting their vision and seeking total control over filming and prodution. The arguments almost scuttled the entire project before the first reel of film had been shot.

Difficulties with Castle Rock

One major disagreement arose over where the movie would be filmed. Castle Rock, in an effort to contain expenses, announced it would film in Toronto, Canada, where cheaper production costs made the enterprise more appealing. Affleck and Damon, who claimed that the "feel" of the harsher Cambridge neighborhoods were essential to the film's impact, vehemently insisted that their movie had to be shot in the Boston area. Castle Rock, footing the bill for production costs, dismissed the argument and let the script lay undeveloped for a time.

A second disagreement arose over who would direct the film. Affleck and Damon wanted to select from a list of ten premier directors, including Martin Scorcese, but Castle Rock executives again asserted the company's right to choose its own director, the relatively unheralded Andrew Scheinman, who had only the 1994 comedy *Little Big League* to his credit. When the two asked Castle Rock to at least send out the script to the ten directors on their list to see if any interest existed, Castle Rock declined.

Like this scene featuring Damon and Robin Williams, much of Good Will Hunting *was filmed in the Cambridge neighborhoods where Affleck and Damon grew up.*

Finally, Castle Rock exercised a contractual option, returning the script to Affleck and Damon, who now had thirty days to locate another studio willing to purchase the rights to the script. If they succeeded, the script remained in their hands. If they could not sign a new agreement, the script reverted to Castle Rock, who could do anything it wanted with the story without Affleck or Damon.

A frenzied race began in November 1995 that offered unthinkable consequences to the two. If they could not locate a savior in thirty short days, all the work they had put into writing *Good Will Hunting* would go down the drain. The movie would be made without them, and their dreams of acting in their own vehicle would collapse.

"Every Single Person . . . Turned It Down"

Four weeks seemed to race by as Affleck and Damon telephoned every production company they could think of, all without result. Potential buyers turned away when they heard the $1 million price for purchasing the script from Castle Rock, which had added the production costs incurred up to that time. Some declined to consider because they had heard rumors that Affleck and Damon were difficult to work with, unknown actors who made demands out of accord with their importance and power. Some studios turned away because they did not believe Affleck and Damon when they contended that the film could be made for less than $10 million.

Affleck says of that difficult November that "every single person, everybody who was in the business of making movies, turned it down. Every single person."[46] The days flew by, each one leaving one less opportunity to rescue their threatened project.

With only three days remaining, luck turned in their favor. Affleck had been working on the film *Chasing Amy*, and decided to show the script to Kevin Smith, the director. Smith took the script home with him that night, read it, and immediately recognized the story's potency. The next morning he contacted Harvey Weinstein, the head of Miramax Studios, and told him he had a script that Weinstein had to read.

After looking at the script, Weinstein immediately concurred with Smith and asked for a meeting with Affleck and Damon. Two

Harvey Weinstein, head of Miramax Studios, purchased the producing rights to Good Will Hunting *from Castle Rock for nearly $1 million.*

days later, only twenty-four hours before rights irrevocably returned to Castle Rock, Weinstein purchased the rights for just under $1 million.

"Harvey really believed in us and told us it was okay to take some more risks, to go with it,"[47] said Affleck. He had seen his dream almost whisked away by one Hollywood studio, only to be salvaged by another. Now he and Damon, assured of having sufficient control over their own script, could turn to making the film version.

"Like a Giant Golden Retriever with a Ball"

Two roles had been filled since the tale's inception. According to their agreement, Matt took the leading role in this film, that of Will Hunting, while Ben would step into the lead role of their second

Meeting Mel Gibson

One of Affleck's most exciting, and frustrating, experiences was meeting Mel Gibson, the multitalented actor and director. One month after Miramax purchased the script to *Good Will Hunting*, Affleck and Matt Damon started driving to Massachusetts for the Christmas holidays. Before they left California, they received a call from Harvey Weinstein, the head of Miramax, informing them that Mel Gibson, fresh from his Oscar-winning work in *Braveheart*, wanted to direct their film. He told them they had a meeting scheduled in New York in two days.

While the pair raced nonstop across the country, they chatted about what this might mean. Their script had been saved only a few weeks earlier, and now one of Hollywood's most powerful individuals wanted to direct the piece. They could hardly believe their good fortune.

Affleck and Damon arrived in time for the meeting. Gibson congratulated the two on their compelling script and stated how he would be excited to direct it. However, since he had already committed to acting in the movie *Ransom*, he could not begin filming *Good Will Hunting* for another year.

A disappointed Affleck and Damon faced a dilemma. An Oscar-winning director wanted to work with them, but they had already waited so long to make their dream materialize on screen. They wanted to start right away. Miramax, as well, had heavily invested in the project and did not want to wait another year before receiving a return.

Affleck and Damon made one of the toughest decisions of their careers and politely declined Gibson's offer. In his book *Matt Damon: An Unauthorized Biography*, author Chris Nickson quotes Damon's explanation for the sudden turn of events: "Mel was totally understanding when we said, 'This movie is our life. And we know you're, like, the biggest star in the world. But we need a decision.'"

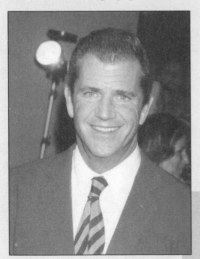

Gus Van Sant later accepted the directing position, but not before Affleck and Damon endured some second-guessing about saying no to a Hollywood legend.

Mel Gibson offered to direct Good Will Hunting, *but scheduling conflicts would have delayed production for an entire year.*

effort. All other parts remained to be cast, especially that of the psychologist who helps Will Hunting, and a director had to be found.

One of Hollywood's most influential figures, actor and director Mel Gibson, read the script and badly wanted to direct. Affleck and Damon were honored that such an accomplished figure would want to be a part of their project, and readily agreed to meet with him. Unfortunately, due to scheduling conflicts Gibson would not be able to work on the film for one year. Eager to push the movie forward, the disappointed pair regretfully told Gibson they could not wait that long.

Ben's brother, Casey, now entered the picture. Busy making his own film, *To Die For*, Casey showed the script to his director, Gus Van Sant. One reading convinced Van Sant that he wanted to direct *Good Will Hunting*. As he told the *Boston Phoenix*, "It was probably the best-written screenplay I had ever read. I wanted to work on it as soon as I closed the last page. It was wonderful. We called it a color-by-numbers script: if you just filled in the scenes as they were written, it would come to life."[48]

Van Sant arranged to meet Affleck to discuss the film. Affleck was so excited about having a quality director that, according to Van Sant, he "was just really, really excited. He was like a giant golden retriever with a ball."[49]

At first Van Sant asked the two to rewrite the script's ending so that Affleck's character, Chuckie, is killed in an accident on a construction site. Though Affleck and Damon told Van Sant the change would add nothing to the story and would only place one more unnecessary burden on Will Hunting, they inserted the scene. After reading the revised version, however, Van Sant agreed it hampered the tale's original flow and told them to keep their story as it was.

More luck flowed their way when Damon landed a leading role in *The Rainmaker*, a courtroom drama based on a popular John Grisham novel and directed by Hollywood legend Francis Ford Coppola. Affleck and Damon believed that if they could time the debut of *Good Will Hunting* to follow shortly after *The Rainmaker*, they could take advantage of the immense publicity that a Coppola film generated.

"Let's See Some I.D."

The third stroke of good fortune arrived when they signed noted actor-comedian Robin Williams to play the part of the psychologist. His inclusion gave credibility to the project and guaranteed the media would pay more attention to the film when it arrived.

Convincing Williams to appear in the film was not hard. He was hooked the first time he read the script and badly wanted to be a part of it. "This is an extraordinary piece," he said, "and the first time I read it I wanted to do it."[50]

Williams knew little about Affleck and Damon, however; not surprisingly, the first time they met, he wondered who these young kids were. Incredulous that such a deeply moving script could be written by two such boyish actors, Williams jokingly asked them when their fathers were arriving and demanded, "Let's see some I.D. [identification]."[51] Affleck and Damon laughed at the remark, then realized that Williams had just paid them a major compliment.

The performance Damon and actress Minnie Driver gave during their audition for Good Will Hunting *was so strong that it moved some observers to tears.*

Affleck and Damon impressed the comedian even more as they got to know each other. Usually, scripts focusing on character changes came from the pens of mature, professional scriptwriters, men and women who had experienced life's trials and tribulations and could use them as material for their writing. These two, however, crafted a powerful script while still young.

Williams was intrigued by "the quality of the writing that these two guys wrote, and then I met them and went, 'Now who wrote this really?' Because you see the depth of perception in the things that they talk about and you go, 'This is something that I want to be part of.'"[52]

Since Williams had other projects scheduled, filming had to begin within five or six weeks. The rest of the cast quickly fell into place. Swedish actor Stellan Skarsgård agreed to play the Harvard professor, and actress Minnie Driver signed on as Will Hunting's girlfriend, Skylar, based on Damon's first serious girlfriend, a medical student named Skylar Satenstein. The chemistry between Damon and Driver was immediate; people observing their audition together were reportedly moved to tears by their performance.

"It's Not a Fluke"

Everything had fallen into place by the spring of 1997. Will Hunting's arduous journey from Affleck's and Damon's imaginations to the written page to the large screen was about to end, as the cast and crew assembled in Cambridge to begin shooting the first scenes. Neither Affleck nor Damon has ever forgotten the tremendous impact that initial day made on them. What could be more perfect? The words they had written were about to be given life by Robin Williams, right in the middle of their childhood neighborhood.

The two nervously watched as Van Sant ordered quiet on the set. Robin Williams, already Oscar-nominated for previous work, launched into his first lines. Affleck and Damon listened intently as the words they had written, in a time that seemed so far away, at last had a sound. The impact carried far more power than they imagined.

"By the time they said 'action' tears were running down my face," explains Damon. "I looked over at Ben, and he was the same way." After completing his lines, Williams noticed how much the moment had meant to the two screenwriters. He walked over to them, placed one hand on each of their heads, and gently remarked, "It's not a fluke; you guys really did it."[53] With those words, the rest of the cast and crew burst into applause for Affleck and Damon.

As the shooting continued through the following weeks, the experience became even more emotional for the two friends. Williams, notorious for improvising his lines instead of religiously adhering to the script, rarely strayed from the moving words his younger cohorts had written. He felt the writing was so strong on its own that he could do little to improve upon it. He related to the emotional center of the film, which he contended received its strength from the intense bond shared by Affleck and Damon.

The two Cambridge actors received further gratification in seeing some of their family and friends play a part in the film. Ben's brother, Casey, played one of Hunting's friends, and one scene contained Affleck's and Damon's parents as well as one of their high school teachers.

They could not have fashioned a more perfect experience. Damon stated that the two almost pinched themselves to make sure that what they were experiencing was no dream. Even if the film failed to garner much praise or attention, they at least had reached their goal. They wrote something, they doggedly insisted on controlling many aspects of the filming, and they watched it come to life on the Cambridge sets.

Robin Williams later stated that no matter how the movie fared at the box office, Affleck and Damon had given the world something unique. He was proud to have been a part of it. "If *Good Will Hunting* makes hundreds of millions of dollars that would be wonderful for the people who invested in it, but for me I got a chance to be in a good movie, to be in a story that has some depth, and that's worth it."[54]

"Rarer than a Breath of Fresh Air"

The movie premiered in Los Angeles in December 1997. Nervous over how their story would fare when pitted against other industry products and when placed before a fickle public, Affleck and

Affleck's brother Casey (upper left) costars in Good Will Hunting *and both Affleck's and Damon's parents make an appearance in the film.*

Damon apprehensively watched the first showing. They then headed to a party that fittingly served bowls of piping hot New England clam chowder and luscious Boston cream pie to them and their friends as they waited for the opening-weekend numbers to tumble in.

They were pleased with the film, but they realized that anything could happen when the public and the critics viewed it. This was their baby, the creation upon which they had labored for so many weeks and months, and they had taken the daunting step of placing their work before the nation and asking people what they thought. Apprehension tore at the young pair.

Their fears dissipated when *Good Will Hunting*, presented on only seven California screens, still pulled in enough money to place nineteenth in the nation. Its per screen average, one of the industry's most valued measuring sticks, stood at number one in the country with $38,897. Theaters sold out wherever the movie was screened. An ecstatic Affleck later mentioned to buddies he felt like someone who had just won the lottery.

Newspaper critics almost universally praised the film for its outstanding story and superb acting. The *Boston Globe* movie critic stated, "Even rarer than a breath of fresh air is a breath of fresh Hollywood film. Brainy and heartfelt and right on target, *Good Will Hunting* is such a film."[55]

The film eventually soared to the top of the box office in the United States and abroad. As *Good Will Hunting* accumulated $226 million worldwide, Affleck and Damon too catapulted to the top.

Elation and Dismay

Industry awards quickly tumbled in as well. In a harbinger that their movie might accumulate even greater honors, Affleck and Damon earned the 1998 Golden Globe Award for best screenplay. In February 1998 Hollywood honored the film by bestowing nine Academy Award nominations on *Good Will Hunting*, including best picture, best director, best supporting actress for Minnie Driver, best original screenplay for Affleck and Damon, best actor for Matt Damon, and best supporting actor for Robin Williams. The work they had put into realizing their dream had succeeded beyond their wildest hopes.

Damon's enthusiasm over receiving a nomination for best actor was dampened by Affleck's failure to receive a similar nod.

He's Not the First, First-Time Winner

When Ben Affleck and Matt Damon won an Oscar for their first screenplay, they matched a standard that few have equaled. However, other movie figures have received an Oscar for their first role or directing debut. Among such winners are some of the entertainment world's most renowned figures. Barbra Streisand won the Best Actress award for her role in *Funny Girl* (1968), and Best Supporting Actress awards went to Anna Paquin for *The Piano* (1993) and Tatum O'Neal for *Paper Moon* (1973).

Three directors took Oscar home after their debut film. In 1980, legendary Robert Redford won for *Ordinary People*, three years before James L. Brooks captured the same honor for *Terms of Endearment*. Kevin Costner matched them in 1990 with his western epic *Dances with Wolves*.

The two had worked closely together and Damon believed they both earned whatever honors came to the picture. He told reporters that Affleck could just as easily have performed in the key role of Will Hunting, but had readily allowed his friend to have that honor.

Their excitement further mellowed when they learned that rumors had surfaced disputing the origin of the script. Malicious stories stated that Affleck and Damon purchased the plot from another writer, that William Goldman had actually written the story, and that the script had already been performed onstage, making it ineligible to receive a nomination for best original screenplay.

Affleck and Damon explained that Goldman had helped them for a day or so, but that the story was theirs from start to finish. They added that while they had performed a small portion of what became the script in Damon's Harvard class, the story had never appeared in a theater or any other business venue.

Their explanations calmed the controversy. An industry committee investigated the matter and concluded that the two had done nothing wrong and that the script was theirs.

"Man, This Is *Crazy!*"

On March 23, 1998, Affleck and Damon walked through the elated crowds packing the street outside the Dorothy Chandler Pavilion in Los Angeles for the Oscar ceremonies. On their arms were two women who most prominently played roles in their lives, their mothers. Affleck said, "It's nice for our moms to see all this stuff; mine even came to the rehearsal and took pictures." He then joked, "She's considering [the Oscar statuette] her grandson, and she's holding it for ransom until she gets her real one."[56]

The two settled into their seats and anxiously waited for their categories to be announced. Host Billy Crystal performed a comical music piece mentioning most nominees, at which Affleck turned to Damon to express his disbelief over where they were. "I remember Billy Crystal did his song montage to open the show, and we were part of it. He was singing, 'Matt and Ben, Ben and Matt,' and I turned to Matt and went, 'Man, this is *crazy!* Surreal!' I mean, we were a joke that people *got*."[57]

Triumph at the Oscars

Ben Affleck and Matt Damon justifiably acted like two young kids when their names were read as winners of the Oscar for best original screenplay. They rushed onstage, where they immediately proceeded to ignore the thirty-second time limit for acceptance speeches in a rambling thank-you to almost everyone who had played a role in their lives, from their mothers to the stagehands working on the film. Instead of impatiently listening to the lengthy speech, the audience responded warmly to the young pair's genuine delight and applauded enthusiastically.

Backstage, reporters swarmed all over the pair, who freely answered every question tossed their way. After completing the round of interviews, the two friends returned to their seats, where they received hugs and congratulations from their mothers, a perfect ending to an extraordinary evening.

Affleck and Damon celebrate after winning the Oscar for best original screenplay at the 1998 Academy Awards.

Damon knew he faced stiff competition for best actor in Jack Nicholson, Dustin Hoffman, and Robert Duvall, and industry analysts predicted a clean sweep for that year's blockbuster, *Titanic*. However, Robin Williams kicked off the evening by capturing the Best Supporting Actor award. After thanking people, he looked at his costars and joked that he still wanted to see some identification from the young screenwriters.

As expected, Damon lost the Best Actor award to Jack Nicholson for his powerful performance in *As Good As It Gets.* The next moments forever altered Affleck's and Damon's lives. When the envelope containing the names of the winner for best original screenplay was opened by Jack Lemmon and Walter Matthau, instead of the favorite, Woody Allen, the presenters read their names. Affleck and Damon jumped onstage, where they proceeded to thank anyone they could think of. "All I know is I staggered up there—it was like this weird out-of-body thing followed by exuberance and screaming my head off,"[58] said Affleck.

The two had realized their dream. In the days to come, Affleck would learn that his world would never be the same. He may have come from a humble Cambridge neighborhood, but he now belonged to the world.

Chapter 6

"He Never Lost His Desire"

THE YEARS FOLLOWING *Good Will Hunting* tested Affleck in many ways. They brought increasing wealth, fame, and attention, but they also brought headaches and problems. What more could he do to top winning an Academy Award? Everything he did from now on would be measured a success or failure according to how the vehicle compared to *Good Will Hunting*. Affleck also struggled to find the proper balance so that he still lived as normal a life as possible. That, he learned, might have been his toughest task.

"A Guy's Guy That Females Love"

It did not take long for Affleck to realize what winning an Oscar meant. The day after receiving the statuette, he and Damon walked into an airport, where they were promptly chased down the corridors by enthusiastic fans. He could no longer walk into the corner drugstore or local mall to purchase personal items, as fans would speedily swarm around him. He told a magazine interviewer that he had "a complete sense of bewilderment and being in a daze. Imagine having to renegotiate your relationship with the entire world."[59]

Many observers in the entertainment world stated that despite his relatively young age, Affleck handled his newfound fame with maturity. He treated fans with respect, signing autographs and posing for pictures in restaurants and other public places whenever he could, because he believed that movie stars had a responsibility to give something back to the people who purchased tickets to their films.

His popularity increased as he appeared in several more successful films. Critics compared him to the industry's top stars, such as Mel Gibson and Tom Cruise. *Biography* magazine stated that "Like Cruise, Harrison Ford, and Mel Gibson, he is the rare star who appeals to both men and women: a guy's guy that females love."[60]

Affleck certainly enjoyed his new wealth; he started purchasing all those things he once could not afford. He moved into a $1.7 million, three-story home in exclusive Hollywood Hills and bought a New York City apartment, five motorcycles, and two Cadillacs, and he filled one room with his favorite video games.

Affleck signs an autograph for a young fan. The actor considers it his responsibility to recognize the fans that have made him the star he is today.

In many ways, Affleck was still the youngster who had grown up in Cambridge—only the storage location for his new toys changed.

"Ben Is One of Those Fearless People"

Fame handed the handsome actor another benefit—beautiful women vied for his attention. Affleck claims he never enjoyed success with girls until this time and that at first the alteration in his personal life perplexed him. Why would a guy who had trouble getting a girl's phone number now have women approach him? As was usually the case in his life, Affleck's Cambridge buddies helped him find perspective.

One time he said to his friends, "I don't know what it is, but things [with women] are really working out for me now." The group he had known since high school looked at each other before one replied, "Uh, it might have something to do with the fact that you're in movies."[61]

Another aspect of Hollywood fame was less fun, however—the swarms of photographers, called paparazzi, who descend on movie stars whenever they appeared in public. Some actors wage battles for their privacy with the photographers, but Affleck tried to make the best of a difficult situation by being amicable. He contends that this is one of the costs of fame and finds it hard to understand why some movie stars try to avoid the press: "It would be like saying, 'Well, I expect to be flown in everywhere for free, I expect to meet the President of the United States, and I expect to get free clothes, but I certainly don't expect to be gossiped about.' I mean, it's clearly all part of the same package."[62]

The gossip publications, called tabloids, have not always been easy for Affleck to accept because they spread many rumors about him and other celebrities. Affleck's easy accessibility has sometimes hurt him, but he has since learned to be a little more circumspect with his statements. He explains that his mother "disapproves of the way I conduct myself in interviews. She thinks I'm too forthcoming and that I talk about my personal life too much."[63]

"He's very business savvy and artistically very opinionated," says actress Sandra Bullock of Affleck. "Ben is one of those fearless people. He has no problem diving into something and say-

Affleck's Popularity

Ben Affleck has enjoyed extraordinary popularity, in the Hollywood community as well as among the general public. Much of it comes from his confident personality and unpretentious image—people want to like him and want to see him succeed.

John Frankenheimer, who directed Affleck in *Reindeer Games*, explained Affleck's popularity to *Biography* magazine in 2000: "He's the closest thing we have today to a Jimmy Stewart. He has a really likable Everyman quality. You root for Ben Affleck. You want him to succeed. I don't think he'd make a good villain."

Jerry Bruckheimer, who produced the high-budget spectacular *Pearl Harbor*, agrees. In a 1999 interview in *Playboy* magazine, Bruckheimer claimed, "Ben's the real thing. He's got that square jaw, that real American look, without being pretty. Women want to be with him and men want to be like him—which is what movie stars are made of."

Affleck accepts the award for favorite movie actor at the 2001 Teen Choice Awards.

ing what he thinks—criticizing people."[64] That is one reason why the national media spread his name all over the front pages when he and Jennifer Lopez played out their relationship in public.

Every Relationship Is a Train Wreck

Affleck's personal problems multiply when the issue concerns women. He has enjoyed few stable relationships since high school, partly because of the media frenzy and partly because he enjoys being single and hanging out with his friends.

A Life on CNN

Sometimes Affleck's celebrity strikes him as surreal. He is accustomed to seeing himself on television—after all, press interviews help promote his work. However, the publicity over his personal life has taken him by surprise. In 1999 he gave an example to writer Zoe Heller of *Harper's Bazaar* magazine:

> To watch updates of your relationships on CNN is bizarre in a way I cannot explain to you. One day, I fell asleep on my couch with the TV on. I was having this dream about everything that was going on in my life [with Gwyneth Paltrow] and when I woke up—there it was—my life was being reported on CNN. CNN! I mean, you think, "Isn't there something happening in Bosnia by God?"

Tabloids have linked his name to women in and out of show business, including singers Mariah Carey and Britney Spears; actresses Pamela Anderson and Sandra Bullock; Chelsea Clinton, the daughter of the former president; and Calista Flockhart, star of the television show *Ally McBeal*, but he has difficulty remaining in a relationship for long. He mentioned to *Us* magazine, "Almost every relationship I've ever been in has basically been a train wreck. I have enough trouble maintaining the even keel in the confines of a normal relationship. I don't expect that to get any easier now that everyone wants a piece of me."[65]

He openly admits that he will fall for a girl, spend time with her, then find some excuse for breaking up. Rather than talking the matter over with the girl, Affleck waits until she does something he dislikes, then uses that as an excuse for calling off the affair. As a result, he tries to keep most women at a distance so he does not have to hurt them or himself. He admits that many women are drawn to him not because of his personality, but because he is a movie star.

The woman with whom he enjoyed the deepest relationship is Oscar-winning actress Gwyneth Paltrow, noted in Hollywood for her golden looks and exceptional talent. The two dated for more than a year, and although they eventually broke up, they have remained friends.

A Quiet Oasis

Whatever steadiness Affleck enjoys in his hectic life comes from the same source that has given him strength and security through the years—his family and his Cambridge friends. That select group has remained constant, and he turns to them to provide a shield from the craziness that Hollywood life offers. Affleck knows they will treat him the same as always, that they will tell him if he is acting like a jerk or doing something wrong. They were there before, and they will be there at every step of the way, whether he has money and fame or whether he is struggling and out of the limelight.

The closest people have been his mother, his brother, Casey, and Matt Damon. While the public correctly views Damon and Affleck as an inseparable pair, Affleck states that Casey is actually his closest friend. The two share not only family background and a Cambridge upbringing, but they live similar professional lives. Casey has been featured in a number of films, including his

Affleck dated Oscar-winning actress Gwyneth Paltrow. Despite breaking up after only one year together, the two remain good friends.

role in *Good Will Hunting*. "We're very close," states Affleck of his brother. "I'm very close with my mom, whom I think is just a saint. She's a superwoman."[66]

These are the individuals to whom Affleck turns whenever turbulence disrupts his life. Women vie for his attention and money gushes in from his string of hit movies, but his family and friends give what he most needs—a quiet, secure oasis. Sometimes Affleck flees to his Cambridge neighborhood to escape the trappings of stardom, while other times he has friends living with him. In both cases Affleck, the down-home guy from a rough Massachusetts neighborhood, gains a shield.

In return, Affleck generously shares the benefits of his acting career with his friends and family. He purchased his mother a beautiful home, and he offers financial help to his friends whenever they need it. Affleck readily hands over the money because he knows his friends will always repay him rather than take advantage of their relationship.

Though he is not family, Matt Damon is an important part of Affleck's inner circle. The two try to hold on to the same lifestyle they enjoyed before becoming famous, which includes playing video games and enjoying Boston Red Sox baseball. Damon states

Affleck (second from right) followed Good Will Hunting *with a role in the 1998 action film* Armageddon. *Starring in a blockbuster cemented Affleck's celebrity status.*

that while many people assume they live wild lives, he and Affleck usually "end up at the same bar every night with the same people telling the same old jokes. We've always been that way."[67]

"I'm Set for Life"

Meanwhile, the success of *Good Will Hunting* brought unimaginable rewards to Affleck. Scripts flowed in from producers, eager to have the popular, good-looking actor in their films. One company even sent him a script calling for the lead to be a black female, but stated that if Affleck were interested, the script would be altered to fit.

His next film, 1998's *Armageddon*, cemented Affleck's status as a star. He accepted the role of A.J. Frost, a cocky oil rigger who joins a crew of men sent into space to stop an asteroid barreling toward Earth. Some people criticized Affleck for taking this big-budget action film, contending that he had forsaken quality movies like *Good Will Hunting* to collect a bigger paycheck. Affleck discounted these claims, explaining that he took the role out of his lifelong love of action films. As a youth he rushed to theaters to watch *Star Wars* and *Back to the Future*, and this was his opportunity to star in a similar movie. This would not be the last time that Affleck accepted a film on the basis of what he thought was right for him, not what others thought for him. In choosing his parts, Affleck relies on his instincts, his gut feelings, his heart.

With *Armageddon* Affleck took loftier aim. For the first time producers provided him with a large trailer on the set, and the six-hundred-thousand-dollar salary made him feel like a king. "I just thought, I'm set for life," he told a magazine reporter. "I've got my 600 bones, and I won't have to do any more [lousy] movies that I don't want to do."[68]

His next selection proved Affleck did not intend to sell out. After *Armageddon*'s triumphant run at the theaters, Affleck could have asked for and received any role he desired in a big budget film. Instead he opted for a smaller film, 1998's *Shakespeare in Love*, a comedy about the famous playwright attempting to deal with writer's block. Affleck accepted the part of Ned Alleyn, a real-life actor in sixteenth-century England, even though some in the business advised him to avoid the role. "Don't do Shakespeare in tights,"[69] argued *Armageddon* producer Michael Bay, who believed that Affleck should build on his performance in the asteroid blockbuster.

Affleck again followed his heart. He loved the script, and he jumped at the chance to join talented actors like Joseph Fiennes and Judi Dench, but mostly he saw it as a chance to prove he could handle his own against such top talent. He liked playing A.J. in *Armageddon*, but felt that many actors could have done a good job in that role. This film, though, delivered a different challenge. He had to perform an English accent and deliver a powerful performance to match Fiennes and Dench.

His tactic worked. Critics praised Affleck, and the film won seven Oscars, including best picture. By taking a role he believed was good for him as an actor, Affleck boosted his professional life. He had written the script for an Oscar-winning movie, acted in a big-budget thriller, and participated in a much-acclaimed film, all within a few years. His future in Hollywood seemed guaranteed.

A Learning Process

For his next three projects, Affleck continued to select his roles carefully, either because the script interested him, or he thought it would be a beneficial career move. He appeared in 1999's romantic comedy *Forces of Nature*, in which he played a man frantically trying to travel to Georgia in time for his wedding, to have the chance to act with Sandra Bullock.

That same year he rejoined Matt Damon and director Kevin Smith to star in the controversial film *Dogma*. He and Damon played a pair of angels banished from heaven who roam the Midwest, making observations on religion. Damon claimed he and Affleck had no difficulty shooting the satire, as "it was easy to fall into playing old buddies who have been kicking around on Earth together for eons, because that's how we feel about each other. We've been through a lot together; we've had some exciting times and some pretty boring ones, so we can imagine spending eternity in Wisconsin together."[70] Affleck did not expect the disputes that marked the film's release to be so acrimonious. Some leaders in the religious community objected to what they viewed

Blunt, but Loveable

Ben Affleck has been called overly candid with the press when discussing his romantic life or his involvement with movies. Actress Sandra Bullock, who costarred with Affleck in the 1999 movie *Forces of Nature*, experienced firsthand that Affleck did not confine his honesty to press interviews. She also learned, though, that he was very personable at the same time.

The first time she met Affleck was at a Los Angeles restaurant, where the two had agreed to have lunch and get to know each other before commencing the filming. At the appointed time, Affleck was nowhere in sight. Finally, thirty minutes tardy, Affleck rushed in and, according to reporter Zoe Heller of *Harper's Bazaar*, without apologizing blurted out, "God, that *Speed 2* [Bullock's most recent film] was a piece of [crap]."

Rather than being insulted by this blunt arrival, Bullock quickly reminded Affleck he had made *Phantoms*, a 1998 movie that met an equally harsh reception from the public. Affleck stopped talking, stared at Bullock for a moment, then grabbed her out of her chair, lifted her up, and hugged her as he swung her in a circle. From that moment on, the two became fast friends.

Affleck and actress Sandra Bullock became close friends after working together in the 1999 movie Forces of Nature.

as an attack on organized religion, but Affleck defended the film and director Kevin Smith, a devout Roman Catholic.

One attitude Affleck exhibited impressed the man he defended, Kevin Smith. Affleck's stock in Hollywood soared in the aftermath of his earlier triumphs, but Affleck remained as unassuming as always. Rather than demand special treatment because he was a major star, Affleck came to work each day with no grand expectations. He just wanted to act.

"No matter how much Ben's star rose during the making of *Dogma*, he never lost his desire to make the film or his belief in it," stated Smith. "Without Ben, I don't think I could have done this movie."[71]

The third film gave Affleck the chance to work with one of Hollywood's great filmmakers. John Frankenheimer had directed some of the most noted stars of the last fifty years, including Paul Newman, and Affleck quickly signed when asked to join the cast of *Reindeer Games*. He figured that he could absorb all sorts of valuable lessons by watching the legend at work.

Affleck's diligence in his approach to the film is typical of how he prepares for a role. Since part of the story takes place in a prison, Affleck spent time in a penitentiary studying the habits of inmates and what the prison system was like. He felt a bit uncomfortable when he and the warden walked through the prison unaccompanied by guards, but learned that the prisoners were just as starstruck as most other people. They readily shared whatever information they possessed about prison, on one condition—they demanded that Affleck describe his affairs with famous women.

As the millennium approached, Affleck enjoyed a prosperous career. He constructed it on a foundation of major star vehicles like *Armageddon*, and smaller projects, like *Dogma*, and would continue to expand in similar fashion in the next four years. They would bring him a mixture of happiness and turmoil.

Chapter 7

"Happiness ...Is Found in the Day-to-Day"

For someone like Ben Affleck, who has succeeded beyond his wildest dreams, the journey is not over. The future holds many opportunities, and he plans to work hard to bring them to fruition. No matter along which path his future meanders, however, Affleck is determined to make it as fulfilling as the rest of his career.

"We Know How Hard It Was"

Now that he has established a stable acting career, Affleck can afford to focus on efforts he earlier had to ignore. It is hardly surprising that Matt Damon is closely involved with many of them.

One of their joint efforts revolves around Pearl Street Productions, a company established to aid aspiring film producers, playwrights, and actors. They know from making *Good Will Hunting* how difficult it is to bring a project to the big screen, so they decided to help those who chose to set out on the path they walked in the 1990s.

Their initial project involved *The Third Wheel*, a screenplay written by Jordan Brady. As Ben recalled, "Jordan had written this screenplay and it was like his *Good Will Hunting*. He'd had offers to buy it, but he wanted to play one of the parts himself and no one would let him because he'd never been cast in anything. Obviously we could appreciate where he was coming from, so we said, 'OK, we'll produce your movie and we'll give you the shot, because we know how hard it was to get our opportunity.'"[72]

Affleck and Damon pose with producer Chris Moore (far left) and writer Pete Jones at a screening of Project Greenlight, *a documentary exploring how a script is made into a movie.*

The pair also signed an agreement with the HBO cable network to develop *Project Greenlight,* a thirteen-episode documentary that takes the viewer through the process of transforming a script into a film. From ten thousand scripts sent in by aspiring filmmakers in an Internet competition, Affleck and Damon selected *Stolen Summer,* by Pete Jones, and with Miramax financial backing, turned the script into a film.

Affleck hopes that these efforts help unknown writers to pursue their dreams. "I hope that young writers are encouraged by us," he told *Biography* magazine in 2002. "And as long as our partners, HBO and Miramax, are ready and willing, we want to keep it going. We want more first-timers to have this great opportunity."[73]

Affleck and Damon kept opening the door for hopefuls in other ways. In June 2000 Affleck and Damon started LivePlanet, a company that seeks to push the boundaries of storytelling and audience participation by using different media, such as the Internet. In one example, they announced plans to develop *Push, Nevada,* a multiepisode series for ABC, involving the disappearance of a large sum of money. Viewers would participate via the Internet to collect clues, then attempt to locate a real cache of money hidden somewhere in the United States.

"The idea of LivePlanet is to change the way you can tell a story, and to change the degree of involvement the audience can have with it," mentioned Affleck. "You have a much higher risk of failure when you're doing something that's never been done before. But that's also the fun of it, the excitement, and to me, the most fulfilling thing I can do in my career."[74]

"We All Wanted to Do It Right"

The subject matter of his next major project, 2001's *Pearl Harbor*, certainly had been made into a movie before, but never on such a grand scale. Affleck wanted to star in the film because he felt he owed a debt to the millions of servicemen who fought in World War II, and to cut costs he agreed to do the movie for a piece of the profit rather than the $10 million salary he then commanded.

"We all did [take a piece of the profit]," he explained shortly after completing work, "because it was not only a great script, but we had a responsibility to tell the stories of these men and women who died for freedom. We all wanted to do it right. I'll only make money if the film makes money."[75]

As he did for *Reindeer Games*, Affleck spent long hours preparing for the role, which required him and the other major stars of the film to endure boot camp. The actors had to run what seemed innumerable miles, wade through swamps, and do hundreds of sit-ups and push-ups. Although the ordeal taxed every actor, Affleck loved it because it challenged him physically and made him feel he was more authentically representing the young pilots stationed at Pearl Harbor in December 1941.

One portion of Affleck's preparation for the film caused great worry on his part. He did not look forward to learning how to fly an aircraft, but once he learned the fundamentals of flight and sat behind the controls of an airplane, he lost his fear.

This film handed Affleck the unique opportunity to learn details of the attack from survivors who were consulted for the filming. Affleck spent hours chatting with the men, and came away with a deep sense of respect for them and the debt owed for what they sacrificed. "The only real message I got from these guys, and they're men of few words, most of the men of that generation, was that they wanted their story told; they want it told well."[76]

While he loved having World War II veterans visiting the set each day, Affleck felt a sense of urgency to complete the film while the aging heroes were alive to see it. "So many of these guys are old now, many of them have passed just from old age. So I felt a sense of urgency just to preserve that [story]. There's only so much oral history you can get and then that generation is gone."[77]

Affleck gained a deep appreciation for what happened during that catastrophic attack on the United States. He was especially humbled by the visit to the *Arizona* Memorial, the monument to the battleship that still rests on Pearl Harbor's bottom, where the men who died aboard it more than sixty years ago are laid to rest. Affleck was honored to be given the chance to participate in a film that so revered these heroes from another generation.

Affleck carefully prepared for his role as a pilot in the 2001 movie Pearl Harbor. *During filming, the actor developed respect for the real-life heroes of the attack.*

The movie, also starring Josh Harnett and Cuba Gooding Jr., became one of the year's top box office attractions. Affleck made money when the film turned a profit, but more importantly to him, the film introduced the heroes of one generation to the young people of another.

The Blockbusters Continue

The following year Affleck starred in a major film based on the popular Tom Clancy novel *The Sum of All Fears*. The film cast Affleck in the role of CIA agent Jack Ryan, a part that had previously been played by two noted actors before him—Alec Baldwin and Harrison Ford. Some people wondered if he should try to fill such large shoes and worried that he would suffer in comparison, but Affleck saw another challenge that he could not let pass.

"What can you do? Just your best and be true to the story," he replied when asked about the inevitable comparisons. He then gave the reason why this role of Jack Ryan so fascinated him—it gave him the chance to portray a younger Ryan and to explore what influences shaped the character:

> This is a different Jack Ryan. He doesn't have all the answers; he doesn't have it all together. He hasn't yet become the U.S. Intelligence superhero. He's starting out, just getting his feet wet. He writes this paper and it takes on a life of its own. That, I could identify with, because that's how it was for me with *Good Will Hunting*. You write something, it takes off, and you're sort of whisked along with it. Ryan's not sure where he'll wind up, where this will lead him, but he's going with it. He's going along for the ride.[78]

Again, the modest superstar gained the respect of others on the set. Director Phil Alden Robinson cited Affleck's willingness to take on a role already identified with other actors as an indication of how confident and secure he felt in his talent. He claimed Affleck worked as hard as anyone and offered support to every member of the crew.

Affleck followed the Tom Clancy story with *Daredevil*, another film that many expected to be a smash success. The profitable

Affleck starred with Jennifer Garner in the box-office failure Daredevil, *based on the comic book of the same name.*

box office take of *Spider-Man* one year earlier had studios scouring comic books for more superheroes, and Twentieth Century Fox thought it found the right one in the story of the Daredevil. The comic book tells the story of Matt Murdock, a blind attorney whose remaining four senses compensated by developing to incredible heights. Each night, Matt Murdock donned his trademark outfit, became Daredevil, and battled crime in the streets of New York City. Affleck, perhaps recalling the hours he spent reading comic books as a youth, was thrilled to be playing a comic book icon.

Though the movie featured a stellar cast, including Colin Farrell and Jennifer Garner, to support Affleck in the central role, it fared poorly. Audiences seemed turned off by the dismally dark sets that marked the entire production, and the movie exited theaters after a brief run.

The Struggle Is More Fun than the Result

Despite the failures of a few films such as *Daredevil*, Ben Affleck has compiled an admirable list of hits. He attributes his success to a number of factors. Rather than sit back and rest on his accomplishments, Affleck continues to do what propelled him to stardom—work hard. He loves the sweat that comes with major projects and never shies from putting in the required time. One of the things that most impresses fellow actors and directors is Affleck's rigorous work ethic: "What's more satisfying is the struggle rather than sitting back and relishing achievement."[79]

Another trademark is his desire to learn. Rather than deciding which roles to take based on the size of the paycheck, Affleck often chooses his endeavors so that he can study the techniques of noted directors or actors. He opted to be the voice of the main character in the cartoon movie *Joseph* so that he could spend time with a famous producer at DreamWorks, Jeffrey Katzenberg, and he looks for other chances to work with legendary figures.

Affleck's assertiveness has also helped him attain the status he now enjoys. Though he has costarred with Hollywood icons, Affleck does not let himself be awed. He offers his opinions on how a role should be performed, and if a director tries to take him from the vision he has selected for the role, Affleck fights for his point of view.

Behind the appealing smile and friendly personality rests a burning desire to be the best. This attitude most appears with his amicable competitiveness toward Matt Damon, with whom he is always matching box office amounts. Affleck constantly pulls for his best friend, as does Damon in return, but Affleck loves to top Damon's accomplishments with one of his own. Affleck, however, does not let that desire interfere with what is most important and contends that "even if my career totally falls apart or I have one of those tragic PR [public relations] disaster things—get arrested with a male hooker or something—or if I just do 15 [lousy] movies and no one wants to hire me again, I still really hope Matt does well."[80]

Rules for Living

When conditions become hectic and Affleck starts to feel the pressures of his job, he remembers three rules for living that he devised when he was starting out as an actor—do not take yourself too seriously, take what you do seriously, and look for the humor in every situation. These informal rules have helped him endure the rougher situations and maintain a positive attitude.

He believes he knows why so many actors have difficulty dealing with fame. He argues that despite their fame and wealth, they are actually not all that happy and do not believe they deserve the acclaim and fortune they have accumulated. He feels that many stars also battle a fear of failure instead of embracing it. Fear of failure provides one of the most potent motivations that he knows.

Industry observers point out that one key to Affleck's accomplishments is that, no matter how well his films fare at the box office or how frequently his image adorns magazines and newspapers, Affleck remains the same individual he was when growing up in Cambridge. A magazine reporter who had known Affleck when he first arrived in California saw him at the Sundance Film Festival after *Good Will Hunting* and was amazed to see Affleck standing in line to get into a movie just like everyone else. He did not expect to avoid the line and walk in before the rest of the crowd, but stood and waited outside, happily chatting with those near him.

However, Affleck has not always enjoyed smooth sailing. Concerned about his excessive drinking, Affleck voluntarily checked into a rehabilitation clinic in 2001. The image of his father's own struggle with alcoholism, which played a prominent part in his parents' divorce, was reminder enough that alcohol abuse could demolish everything he had so carefully constructed over the last fifteen years.

To the Future

Affleck expects the years ahead to be as bright as the ones through which he has just emerged. First of all, he has learned from everything he has experienced, including those difficult early years when he and Damon struggled to earn a living. "I'm glad I spent enough time out there making a living and being an actor but totally under the radar," he explained to *Biography* magazine:

> I could see people's careers evolve and how they handled it. It's a valuable thing to watch and I think it prepared me. All of a sudden you are on the cover of magazines and getting all these movies and you're in the position of losing out on things because you don't have enough time.
>
> But I also appreciate it. It is a little hectic and crazy, but it's certainly better than sitting around your house, waiting for the phone to ring.[81]

The Boston Red Sox

As do many who grow up in the Boston area, Ben Affleck developed an intense devotion to the city's baseball team, the Boston Red Sox. He has suffered and rejoiced in their exploits and failures through the years, so much so that he and Matt Damon included a hilarious and touching scene in *Good Will Hunting* in which the psychologist, played by Robin Williams, explains to Will Hunting that he met his future wife on the night of a famous Red Sox World Series game. When he mentions that he gave up his ticket to the game, Will Hunting reacts in disbelief. How could anyone pass on the Red Sox just to meet a girl, he wonders.

Ben Affleck can relate to those words, which he helped write. The Red Sox have been a continual source of frustration through the years due

to their inability to win a World Series. In the 2003 postseason contests, which included the Red Sox, Affleck was frequently seen in the stands of Boston's Fenway Park.

Affleck enjoys a Boston Red Sox game with girlfriend Jennifer Lopez. Affleck has been a loyal Sox fan since childhood.

He understands that his movies will not always please everyone, so he does what makes him feel right. "You can't please everybody," he mentioned. "You can only make a movie that you're proud of, and hope for the best."[82]

Affleck has few rigid goals for the future. If possible, he would like to act in a western, a film genre he has loved since childhood, but it is not a driving factor. He feels that he will gradually be involved in fewer major projects that place him squarely in the spotlight and will, instead, labor more behind the scenes.

The Future

Ben Affleck looks to the future with much optimism and anticipation. He does not know what the years hold in store but gave this prediction to *Biography* magazine in 2002:

> If I were to guess what the next 10 years of my life would be, I would think they'd involve less acting, particularly the kind of acting that requires you to do a bunch of publicity, the kind that changes the quality of your life as a person. Eventually, I think I'll tone down the degree to which I expose my whole life to the world and put myself out there. If I was doing less than that, I feel it would be more conducive to settling down, getting married, and having a family. That's important to me.

In the meantime, wherever his career heads, he intends to enjoy the process, for he long ago understood that the journey brings more satisfaction than the end result:

> I think what's important is the journey not the destination, because there isn't really a destination. That's a myth. It's like you ascribe this meaning to some finish line point and you say, "If I could just get there, I'll be happy, everything will be OK." But those places don't really exist. I accomplished some of the things that I wanted to accomplish, and I thought those things were gonna make me happy. They didn't, and I was confused by that, until I realized I was looking in the wrong place. Happiness, I think, is found in the day-to-day, and who you are when you wake up, regardless of what you're trying to achieve, or have achieved. And at the end of the day, your work speaks for itself.[83]

Notes

Introduction: "I Value All Those Guys More"

1. Quoted in Tom Gliatto, "Under Pressure," *People*, August 18, 2003, p. 59.
2. Quoted in Gliatto, "Under Pressure," p. 59.
3. Quoted in Joel Achenbach, "Bennifer: Why Are We Hoping for a Flop?" *Washington Post*, August 13, 2003, p. C8.
4. Quoted in Joey Bartolomeo, "Ben & J. Lo's Big Trouble?" *Us*, August 18, 2003, p. 46.
5. Quoted in Joey Bartolomeo, "J. Lo's Broken Heart," *Us*, September 29, 2003, p. 49.
6. Quoted in Bernard Weinraub, "Interview with Ben Affleck," *Playboy*, December 1999, p. 17.

Chapter 1: "The Coolest Thing I've Ever Seen"

7. Quoted in Sheryl Berk, "Ben Affleck on Stardom, Settling Down, and Working with Best Buddy Matt Damon," *Biography*, July 2002, p. 38.
8. Quoted in Kitty Bowe Hearty, "Ben Affleck: A Guy's Guy That Women Love," *Biography*, February 2000, p. 58.
9. Quoted in Luaine Lee, "The Summer's Hottest Superhero on Love, Motorcycles, and Living in a *Jerry Springer* Universe," E! Online, 1998. www.eonline.com/Celebs/Qa/Affleck/index.html.
10. Quoted in Hearty, "Ben Affleck," p. 58.
11. Quoted in Berk, "Ben Affleck on Stardom," p. 39.

Chapter 2: "Matt and I Had Identical Interests"

12. Quoted in *Biography Today*, "Ben Affleck," September 1999, p. 11.

13. Quoted in *Biography Today*, "Ben Affleck," p. 11.
14. Quoted in *Biography Today*, "Ben Affleck," p. 11.
15. Quoted in *Biography Today*, "Ben Affleck," p. 11.
16. Quoted in *Biography Today*, "Ben Affleck," p. 12.
17. Quoted in Sheryl Altman, *Matt Damon and Ben Affleck On and Off the Screen*. New York: HarperCollins, 1998, p. 12.
18. Quoted in Berk, "Ben Affleck on Stardom," p. 40.
19. Quoted in Weinraub, "Interview with Ben Affleck," p. 12.
20. Quoted in Weinraub, "Interview with Ben Affleck," p. 17.
21. Quoted in Lee, "The Summer's Hottest Superhero."
22. Quoted in Ingrid Sischy, "Interview with Matt Damon and Ben Affleck," *Interview*, December 1997, p. 3.
23. Quoted in Sischy, "Interview with Matt Damon and Ben Affleck," p. 3.
24. Quoted in Weinraub, "Interview with Ben Affleck," pp. 11–12.
25. Quoted in Hearty, "Ben Affleck," p. 59.

Chapter 3:
"There's a Side of You That People Really Haven't Seen"

26. Quoted in Berk, "Ben Affleck on Stardom," p. 40.
27. Quoted in *Biography Today*, "Ben Affleck," p. 13.
28. Quoted in Weinraub, "Interview with Ben Affleck," p. 8.
29. Quoted in *Biography Today*, "Ben Affleck," pp. 13–14.
30. Quoted in Altman, *Matt Damon and Ben Affleck On and Off the Screen*, p. 32.
31. Quoted in Hearty, "Ben Affleck," p. 59.
32. Quoted in Weinraub, "Interview with Ben Affleck," p. 14.
33. Quoted in Hearty, "Ben Affleck," p. 57.
34. Weinraub, "Interview with Ben Affleck," p. 4.

Chapter 4: "We'd Just Make This Movie Ourselves"

35. Quoted in Altman, *Matt Damon and Ben Affleck On and Off the Screen*, p. 54.
36. Quoted in Sischy, "Interview with Matt Damon and Ben Affleck," p. 7.
37. Quoted in Sischy, "Interview with Matt Damon and Ben Affleck," p. 5.

38. Quoted in *Biography Today*, "Ben Affleck," p. 15.

39. Quoted in *Biography Today*, "Ben Affleck," p. 15.

40. Quoted in Deborah Russell, "Interview with Ben Affleck," Launch Online. www.geocities.com/affleck1971/launch.html.

41. Quoted in Airman, *Matt Damon and Ben Affleck On and Off the Screen*, p. 56.

42. Quoted in Chris Nickson, *Matt Damon: An Unauthorized Biography*. Los Angeles: Renaissance, 1999, p. 88.

43. Quoted in Sischy, "Interview with Matt Damon and Ben Affleck," p. 9.

44. Quoted in Sischy, "Interview with Matt Damon and Ben Affleck," p. 9.

45. Quoted in Altman, *Matt Damon and Ben Affleck On and Off the Screen*, p. 65.

Chapter 5: "You Guys Really Did It"

46. Quoted in Weinraub, "Interview with Ben Affleck," p. 15.

47. Quoted in Berk, "Ben Affleck on Stardom," p. 40.

48. Quoted in Altman, *Matt Damon and Ben Affleck On and Off the Screen*, p. 66.

49. Quoted in *Biography Today*, "Ben Affleck," p. 17.

50. Quoted in Jay David, *The Life and Humor of Robin Williams*. New York: Quill, 1999, p. 204.

51. Quoted in David, *The Life and Humor of Robin Williams*, p. 200.

52. Quoted in Andy Dougan, *Robin Williams*. New York: Thunder's Mouth, 1998, p. 230.

53. Quoted in Nickson, *Matt Damon*, p. 139.

54. Quoted in Dougan, *Robin Williams*, p. 234.

55. Quoted in Ron Givens, *Robin Williams: A Biography*. New York: Time, 1999, p. 121.

56. Quoted in Altman, *Matt Damon and Ben Affleck On and Off the Screen*, p. 99.

57. Quoted in Berk, "Ben Affleck on Stardom," p. 41.

58. Quoted in Berk, "Ben Affleck on Stardom," p. 41.

Chapter 6: "He Never Lost His Desire"

59. Quoted in Weinraub, "Interview with Ben Affleck," p. 4.

60. Quoted in Hearty, "Ben Affleck," p. 57.

61. Quoted in Lee, "The Summer's Hottest Superhero."

62. Quoted in Zoe Heller, "Sandra Bullock & Ben Affleck—Two for the Road," *Harper's Bazaar*, April 1999, p. 5.

63. Quoted in Heller, "Sandra Bullock & Ben Affleck," p. 5.

64. Quoted in Heller, "Sandra Bullock & Ben Affleck," p. 4.

65. Quoted in Altman, *Matt Damon and Ben Affleck On and Off the Screen*, p. 89.

66. Quoted in Lee, "The Summer's Hottest Superhero."

67. Quoted in Sischy, "Interview with Matt Damon and Ben Affleck," p. 6.

68. Quoted in Weinraub, "Interview with Ben Affleck," p. 3.

69. Quoted in Weinraub, "Interview with Ben Affleck," p. 16.

70. Quoted in Hearty, "Ben Affleck," p. 104.

71. Quoted in Hearty, "Ben Affleck," p. 104.

Chapter 7: "Happiness . . . Is Found in the Day-to-Day"

72. Quoted in Nigel Floyd, "Interview with Ben Affleck," My Movies.Net. www.geocities.com/affleck1971/mymovie.html.

73. Quoted in Berk, "Ben Affleck on Stardom," p. 40.

74. Quoted in Berk, "Ben Affleck on Stardom," p. 40.

75. Quoted in Paul Fischer, "Star Talk," Cranky Critic. www.geo cities.com/affleck1971/cranky.html.

76. Quoted in "Affleck Talks *Pearl Harbor*," Mr. Showbiz, May 25, 2001, www.geocities.com/affleck1971/mrshowbiz2.html.

77. Quoted in Jordon Reife, "Ben Affleck on Bounce," Popcorn. www.geocities.com/affleck1971/popcorn1.html.

78. Quoted in Berk, "Ben Affleck on Stardom," p. 99–100.

79. Quoted in Veronica Mixon, "The Buck-Naked Truth on Body Doubles, Jail Time, and Keeping It Real with Charlize," E! Online, 2000. www.eonline.com/Celebs/Qa/Affleck2000.

80. Quoted in Weinraub, "Interview with Ben Affleck," p. 18.

81. Quoted in Hearty, "Ben Affleck," p. 104.

82. Quoted in Berk, "Ben Affleck on Stardom," p. 38.

83. Quoted in Floyd, "Interview with Ben Affleck," p. 2.

Important Dates in the Life of Ben Affleck

1972
Benjamin Geza Affleck is born in Oakland, California, on August 15.

1977
The Affleck family moves to Cambridge, Massachusetts.

1978
Affleck appears in a Burger King television commercial.

1979
Affleck appears in his first film, *The Dark End of the Street*.

1980
Affleck meets the ten-year-old Matt Damon; he appears in the PBS series *The Voyage of the Mimi*.

1984
Affleck's parents divorce.

1986
Signs to play a key role in the ABC after-school special, *Wanted: The Perfect Guy*.

1987
Appears in the television miniseries, *Hands of a Stranger;* he signs to act in the movie *Aluk*, which shuts down before production starts.

1990
Enters the University of Vermont.

1991
Enters Occidental College; he appears in the television movie *Danielle Steele's Daddy*.

1992
Appears in *School Ties;* he and Damon act out a scene of Damon's college script in a Harvard class.

1993
Appears in *Dazed and Confused* and *Against the Grain.*

1994
Affleck and Damon sell the script for *Good Will Hunting* to Castle Rock Entertainment.

1995
Appears in *Mallrats;* meets director Kevin Smith; Miramax purchases the rights to the *Good Will Hunting* script.

1997
Appears in *Chasing Amy, Going All the Way,* and in *Good Will Hunting.*

1998
Affleck and Damon win the Golden Globe Award for best screenplay and the Academy Award for best original screenplay; Affleck appears in *Armageddon* and *Shakespeare in Love.*

1999
Appears in *Forces of Nature, Dogma,* and *200 Cigarettes.*

2000
Appears in *Reindeer Games,* and lends his voice to the animated *Joseph;* he and Damon form LivePlanet.

2001
Meets Jennifer Lopez; appears in *Pearl Harbor.*

2002
Appears in *The Sum of All Fears* and *Changing Lanes.*

2003
Appears in *Daredevil, Gigli* with Jennifer Lopez, and *Paycheck;* he and Lopez break their engagement.

For Further Reading

Books

Mark Bego, *Matt Damon: Chasing a Dream*. Kansas City: Andrews McMeel, 1998. Bego's well-written biography, intended for the upper elementary school market, delivers a fine combination of text and photographs of Ben Affleck's closest friend.

Sam Wellman, *Ben Affleck*. Philadelphia: Chelsea House, 2001. The slim book provides a brief survey of the actor's life, and focuses on the time leading up to and including *Good Will Hunting*.

Periodicals

Rosie Amodio, "50 Things You Never Knew About Ben Affleck," *YM*, February 1999.

Maureen Basura, "Ben and Casey Affleck," *Teen*, July 1998.

Scott Bowles, "Star-Couple Comedies Die Laughing," *USA Today*, August 4, 2003.

Terry Lawson, "Of Cash and Christ and CD Swapping," *Detroit Free Press*, September 21, 2003.

Claudia Puig, "*Gigli:* It's Hard to Pronounce, and Harder to Fathom," *USA Today*, August 1, 2003.

Sam Wloszczyna and Ann Oldenburg, "Why Ben & Jen Still Sit Pretty," *USA Today*, August 1, 2003.

Internet Sources

Lisa Canning, "News Askew," Entertainment Tonight Online.

www.geocities.com/affleck1971/newsaskew.html. This brief interview with Ben Affleck contains his thoughts about the films he made after *Good Will Hunting.*

Jim Ferguson, "Interview with Ben Affleck," StudioLA. www.geocities.com/Affleck1971/studiola.html. Ben Affleck talks about war veterans and the impact of making the film *Pearl Harbor.*

Paul Fischer, "Star Talk," Cranky Critic. www.geocities.com/affleck1971/cranky.html. Ben Affleck shares his opinions on a variety of topics, including his relationship with the press.

Art Jahnke, Interview with Ben Affleck," Darwin. www.geocities.com/affleck1971/darwin.html. The interviewer, a personal friend, asks Affleck numerous questions about the role of computerized technology in the film industry.

Ellen A. Kim, "Ben Affleck's Pearls of Wisdom," Hollywood.com, May 18, 2001. www.geocities.com/affleck1971/hollywood.html. Affleck explains why the film *Pearl Harbor* meant so much to him and why the nation owes a debt to war veterans.

Jordon Reife, "Ben Affleck on Bounce," Popcorn. www.geocities.com/affleck1971/popcorn1.html. Ben Affleck shares his views on actors' preparation for movies and his own film, *Pearl Harbor.*

———, "Ben Behaving Badly" Popcorn. www.geocities.com/affleck1971/popcorn2.html. The writer talks to Ben Affleck about working with revered director John Frankenheimer.

Andrew Rodgers, Don't Rain on Ben Affleck's Parade at "Pearl Harbor," Zap2it.com, May 24, 2001. www.geocities.com/affleck1971/zap2it.html. Background information about the making of *Pearl Harbor.*

Wendy Wilson, "Interview with Ben Affleck," Roughcut. www.geocities.com/affleck1971/roughcut.html. This interview covers Affleck's work on the film *Chasing Amy.*

Works Consulted

Books

Sheryl Altman, *Matt Damon and Ben Affleck On and Off the Screen*. New York: HarperCollins, 1998. This brief biography does not dig deeply into Ben Affleck's life, but adequately covers how he and Matt Damon cowrote the script of *Good Will Hunting*.

Jay David, *The Life and Humor of Robin Williams*. New York: Quill, 1999. This biography of Williams contains some interesting information on life in Hollywood and on the making of *Good Will Hunting*.

Maxine Diamond with Harriet Hemmings, *Matt Damon: A Biography*. New York: Pocket, 1998. This easy-to-read biography is a good place to start in learning about Matt Damon's relationship with Ben Affleck.

Andy Dougan, *Robin Williams*. New York: Thunder's Mouth, 1998. This in-depth look at comedian-actor Robin Williams offers a delightful account of his work with Ben Affleck for *Good Will Hunting*.

Ron Givens, *Robin Williams: A Biography*. New York: Time, 1999. Givens includes some good information on *Good Will Hunting* in this excellent life story of Robin Williams.

Chris Nickson, *Matt Damon: An Unauthorized Biography*. Los Angeles: Renaissance, 1999. Nickson includes some helpful information about Ben Affleck in this readable biography of Matt Damon, especially pertaining to the writing and selling of the script of *Good Will Hunting*.

Periodicals

Joel Achenbach, "Bennifer: Why Are We Hoping for a Flop?" *Washington Post*, August 13, 2003.

Joey Bartolomeo, "Ben & J. Lo's Big Trouble?" *Us*, August 18, 2003.

———, "J. Lo's Broken Heart," *Us*, September 29, 2003.

Sheryl Berk, "Ben Affleck on Stardom, Settling Down, and Working with Best Buddy Matt Damon," *Biography*, July 2002.

Biography Today, "Ben Affleck," September 1999.

Tom Gliatto, "Under Pressure," *People*, August 18, 2003.

Kitty Bowe Hearty, "Ben Affleck: A Guy's Guy That Women Love," *Biography*, February 2000.

Zoe Heller, "Sandra Bullock & Ben Affleck—Two for the Road," *Harper's Bazaar*, April 1999.

Ingrid Sischy, "Interview with Matt Damon and Ben Affleck," *Interview*, December 1997.

Bernard Weinraub, "Interview with Ben Affleck," *Playboy*, December 1999.

Internet Sources

"Affleck Talks *Pearl Harbor*," Mr. Showbiz, May 25, 2001. www.geocities.com/affleck1971/mrshowbiz2.html.

Nigel Floyd, "Interview with Ben Affleck," My Movies.Net. www.geocities.com/affleck1971/mymovie.html.

Anderson Jones, "On Two-Timing Friends, Facing Fame, and Busting His Hump in Boot Camp," E! Online. www.eonline. com.

Luaine Lee, "The Summer's Hottest Superhero on Love, Motorcycles, and Living in a *Jerry Springer* Universe," E! Online, 1998. www.eonline.com/Celebs/Qa/Affleck/index. html.

Veronica Mixon, "The Buck-Naked Truth on Body Doubles, Jail Time, and Keeping It Real with Charlize," E! Online, 2000. www.eonline.com/Celebs/Qa/Affleck2000.

Deborah Russell, "Interview with Ben Affleck," Launch Online. www.geocities.com/affleck1971/launch.html.

Jeffery Wells, "Affleck Prophesies *Dogma* Controversy," Mr. Showbiz, July 2, 1998. www.geocities.com/affleck1971/mr showbiz1.html.

Web Site

Daredevil the Movie (www.daredevil-movies.com). This site contains numerous nuggets of information about the Ben Affleck film and the actors involved in it.

Index

Picture Credits

About the Author

John F. Wukovits is a junior high school teacher and writer from Trenton, Michigan, who specializes in history and biography. Besides biographies of Anne Frank, Jim Carrey, Michael J. Fox, Stephen King, and Martin Luther King Jr. for Lucent, he has written biographies of the World War II commander Admiral Clifton Sprague, Barry Sanders, Tim Allen, Jack Nicklaus, Vince Lombardi, and Wyatt Earp. He is also the author of many books about World War II, including the July 2003 book, *Pacific Alamo: The Battle for Wake Island*. A graduate of the University of Notre Dame, Wukovits is the father of three daughters—Amy, Julie, and Karen.